TIMELESS WISDOM
ON
Overcoming Fear

TIMELESS WISDOM
ON
Overcoming Fear

COMPILED BY
WARREN W. WIERSBE

KREGEL
CLASSICS

Timeless Wisdom on Overcoming Fear
compiled by Warren W. Wiersbe

Published by Kregel Publications, a division of Kregel Inc., 2450 Oak Industrial Dr. NE, Grand Rapids, MI 49505. All rights reserved.

Previously published as *Classic Sermons on Overcoming Fear.*

Library of Congress Cataloging-in-Publication Data
Classic Sermons on Overcoming Fear/ compiled by Warren W. Wiersbe.
p.cm.-{Kregel classic sermons series) Includes biographical references and index.
1.Prayer-Sermons. 2. Sermons, English. I. Wiersbe, Warren. II. Series.
BV4908.5.C53   1991   248.8'6—dc20   91-11868

ISBN 978-0-8254-4855-3

CONTENTS

SCRIPTURE TEXT INDEX

PREFACE

This series is an attempt to assemble and publish meaningful sermons from master preachers about significant themes.

These are *sermons*, not essays or chapters taken from books about themes. Not all of these sermons could be called "great," but all of them are *meaningful*. They apply the truths of the Bible to the needs of the human heart, which is something that all effective preaching must do.

While some are better known than others, all of the preachers, whose sermons I have selected, had important ministries and were highly respected in their day. The fact that a sermon is included in this volume does not mean that either the compiler or the publisher agrees with or endorses everything that the man did, preached, or wrote. The sermon is here because it has a valued contribution to make.

These are sermons about *significant* themes. The pulpit is no place to play with trivia. The preacher has thirty minutes in which to help mend broken hearts, change defeated lives, and save lost souls; and he can never accomplish this demanding ministry by distributing homiletical tidbits. In these difficult days, we do not need "clever" pulpiteers who discuss the times; we need dedicated ambassadors who will preach the eternities.

The reading of these sermons can enrich your own spiritual life. The studying of them can enrich your own skills as an interpreter and expounder of God's truth. However God uses these sermons in your own life and ministry, my prayer is that His Church around the world will be encouraged and strengthened.

WARREN W. WIERSBE

The Delight of Danger

Victor Raymond Edman (1900-1967) served as a missionary to the Quechua Indians in Ecuador from 1923 to 1928 when poor health forced him home. He pastored in Massachusetts for six years and then taught for one year at Nyack Missionary Training Institute in New York. From 1936 to 1940, he taught political science at Wheaton (Illinois) College. He was named president in 1940 and became chancellor in 1965. He died suddenly in 1967 while giving a message in the chapel building named in his honor. He was a popular conference speaker and authored many inspiring devotional books.

This sermon was given in Chicago at the Forty-Eighth Annual Moody Bible Institute Founder's Week Conference, February 1, 1954, and was published in the book of Founder's Week messages. It is used by permission of The Moody Bible Institute.

Victor Raymond Edman

1

THE DELIGHT OF DANGER

Blessed is the man that feareth the Lord, that delighteth greatly in his commandments (Psalm 112:1).

USING PSALM 112 for our meditation for this hour, we seem to have at the outset a contradiction in terms. Blessed or happy is not characteristic of someone who is afraid.

The term "fear," when it applies to the Almighty, is not one of dread or apprehension, but rather of awe, reverence, and the utmost respect. In the Scriptures the word "fear" often does mean apprehension or concern; but we are taught that perfect love casts out fear (1 John 4:18), that is, love for God will cancel out the fear which may be in our heads and hearts. So it is here, that fear of the Lord, the reverence, the utmost of respect, the sense of deep awe that we have or should have for the Almighty, will cancel out other fears which might come into our experience.

In verse 2 the psalmist begins to enumerate some of these fears. The first one which the fear of God will cancel out is the fear we have for our loved ones. "His seed shall be mighty upon earth: the generation of the upright shall be blessed." The children of the godly, says the Word of God, shall be blessed.

No concern goes deeper into the human heart than the apprehension for one's own. Suppose we consider this from two possible points of view. First of all from that of the children, and then from that of the parents.

The Children's View

As to the children, may I say that the greatest blessing you can be to your father and mother is to be a believer in the Lord Jesus Christ, your heart utterly dedicated to Him. It is quite possible that though we are believers in

9

the Lord Jesus we are sometimes thoughtless about our parents. If you have your mother and your father, you can be thankful. They will not always be here. These then are the days when you can be a source of great joy and blessing to them.

The late Dr. George W. Truett, of Dallas, used to tell this little life story about a friend of his. This friend said to Dr. Truett, "You know, George, when I was a boy out on the farm, my father was stricken with a cardiac condition, so that for quite a time he was unable to do any work on the farm. I used to think it was kind of rough on me to come home from school, get into old clothes and overalls and go out in the barn to do the chores, or to be working on the farm all summer long.

"But one afternoon as I had come in and changed my clothes and was going out to the barn for the chores, I stopped for a moment to talk with my dad. He was sitting by the window in his large easy chair, looking out across the farm. He told me this and that which I should be sure to do. Then looking up at me he said, 'Jim, you've been a good son to me. You've been so faithful and so helpful.' I appreciated those words and said, 'Thank you, Dad,' and went out to my work. Those were the last words my dad ever spoke, and all down the years they have rung in my ears, 'You've been a good boy to me.'"

So I come with a particular plea out of the Word of God about obeying parents and honoring father and mother, because now is your opportunity, and there'll not always be that opportunity.

Let me add another thought on that point. It may be that your dad is unsaved. If so, you have a particular concern for his salvation, and therefore you will need to be very thoughtful and considerate and consistent. There is a tendency oftentimes for a young person whose father is not a Christian, to let him be by himself, because there seems to be so little in common.

Several years ago one of our Wheaton lassies came to me at the end of her school year. I knew her even before she came to college. She said, "I don't know where to go after commencement day. The Lord hasn't opened any door for me as yet." I said, "Cheryl, let's pray about that," and so we did. After we had our prayer together, I said, "You know, I think you ought to go home for a while. That dear dad of yours is not a Christian. I have a lot of respect and affection for him. He's always very gracious and courteous to me when I visit in the home. I know he's deeply attached to you and to your sister, and yet he stands outside the fold. If I were you I would get a job close at hand and live at home, and love your dad and show your appreciation to him."

Last fall her younger sister came to me one afternoon, and said, "My daddy's just been saved. Mother called me on the phone and told me." I don't know all the details, but I do now there's a relationship between the love of Christian young people and their devotion and honor to parents, and the coming of these parents to a saving knowledge of the Lord Jesus.

Since the deep awakening God was pleased to send to us at the college a few years ago, I've had hundreds of parents tell me what it meant to them. For instance, a mother and father in California said to me some weeks after we had that deep stirring of heart, "We wouldn't take a million dollars for the phone call that we received from Wheaton the night of that awakening. Our freshman girl called and said, 'Mom, you know I haven't slept tonight, because I've been so ungrateful to you and Daddy.'" That girl hadn't committed any great sin by human standards. She hadn't killed anybody or robbed a college or anything of that kind. She had been ungrateful to her father and mother, and didn't get any rest of heart or any sleep until that was made right.

From the Parents' Point of View

Not only on the part of you children do I make this appeal, but also on the part of parents. You may rest with quiet confidence that "the generation of the upright shall be blessed." Share with me the experience of one lad, a few years ago now, who gave us a testimony in chapel. He said, "I came here unsaved, but in my freshman year I received Christ as my Savior. After that service I went up to my room and wrote a note to my mother and told her about it. My mother is Norwegian by background, and though she would usually write me in English, if she was disturbed she would write partly in Swedish, but if she was very deeply stirred she would write in Norwegian. When I received her reply to my letter telling her I had received Christ, some of the words were Swedish, but most of them were Norwegian, and many of them I couldn't read at all—they were blotted out by tears." That's how Torrey Johnson was saved, and his mother's heart attitude about it.

There is an eye that sees, a heart that feels, and an arm that is not shortened that it cannot reach out and save. So then you may have this confidence, "Blessed is the one that feareth the Lord." Fearing God will cancel out the fear that you have for your dear ones.

There is another fear mentioned in verse 4: "Unto the upright there ariseth light in the darkness." All of us are afraid of being in the dark, if there is uncertainty around us.

Just a year ago I was in the far interior of Liberia, West Africa, for a brief time, visiting missionaries and helping to set up a new missionary project. The first night in the little mud hut where I was being entertained, the generator stopped and the lights went out. The gasoline had given out, and there would be no light unto morning. I was resting and relaxing underneath the mosquito net covering the bed, when all of a sudden I was conscious of the fact that there was something on the floor. Now, the missionary children had been telling that they had seen some men with a big black or green Cobra. It was so dark in my room I couldn't see my fingers in front of my face, but I could hear something on the floor underneath my bed. While I was listening, I inadvertently put the sole of my foot against the mosquito net and something touched my foot.

Just outside the mosquito netting was a little flashlight my wife had sent with me. Should I lift the netting and reach out in the darkness for that light? Finally I did, and flashing the light I discovered it was not a snake, but a great big rat. Because I was no longer concerned, I slept the rest of the night in perfect calmness.

But how darkness distorts things and fills our hearts with apprehension. The Word of God says, "Unto the upright there ariseth light in the darkness"—not after the darkness is gone, but in the midst of it. Said the Lord Jesus, "I am the light of the world: he that followeth me shall not walk in darkness, but shall have the light of life" (John 8:12). Following Him, with the Light before us, we walk in His light. But if we turn away from Him, then we walk in darkness, the darkness of our own shadow.

That may be the reason for the darkness which surrounds your soul today. It may be that disobedience, unwillingness, stubbornness, or rebellion against God's dealings with you is the cause of that shadow. Just where you are right now, turn back to the Lord. He is the Light of the world, and turning to Him you will have light on the way you should take.

Or the darkness may come even without disobedience. Said Isaiah, "Who is there among you that feareth the Lord, that obeyeth the voice of his servant, that walketh in darkness, and hath no light?" (50:10). It is possible that the enemy may cast darkness across our pathway. What are we to do then? "Let him trust in the name of the Lord, and stay upon his God."

If you are walking to the best of your ability in the center of God's will and suddenly there comes darkness into your experience, uncertainty as to what to do, and apprehension fills your heart, then stand still and see the salvation of the Lord. The Word says, "Unto the upright there ariseth light in the darkness."

That light may come through some other Christian. Paul said, "God, who lifteth up those who are cast down in heart, encouraged us by the coming of Titus" (2 Cor. 7:6). Or it may come in the Word of God, much as it came to Paul that night after days and nights on that little ship, on his journey to Rome. So through some believer filled with God's Spirit, or through the Word which is a lamp unto our feet, light will arise in the darkness of our hearts, and the fear of God will cancel out the fear of darkness.

Another fear is mentioned in verse 7 of Psalm 112: "He shall not be afraid of evil tidings: his heart is fixed, trusting in the Lord." Who is not afraid of evil tidings that come suddenly? You know what it is to have the telephone ring after midnight, or to receive a special delivery letter, or to return home and find a notice that Western Union has a message for you, or to get an unexpected long distance call.

But the Word of God says, "Ye shall not be afraid of evil tidings." Whatever may arise, regardless of how suddenly it may come, not afraid? Why? Because he has put the fear of God in his heart, and that has canceled out the fear of sudden tidings.

These are some of the fears from which God delivers us. We are reminded of the word in Psalm 34:4 which says, "I sought the Lord, and he heard me, and delivered me from all my fears."

Notes

Fearing and Trusting—Trusting and Not Fearing

Charles Haddon Spurgeon (1834-1892) is undoubtedly the most famous minister of modern times. Converted in 1850, he united with the Baptists and soon began to preach in various places. He became pastor of the Baptist church in Waterbeach in 1851, and three years later he was called to the decaying Park Street Church, London. Within a short time, the work began to prosper, a new church was built and dedicated in 1861, and Spurgeon became London's most popular preacher. In 1855, he began to publish his sermons weekly; and today they make up the fifty-seven volumes of *The Metropolitan Tabernacle Pulpit*. He founded a pastor's college and several orphanages.

This sermon is taken from *The Metropolitan Tabernacle Pulpit*, volume 59.

Charles Haddon Spurgeon

2

FEARING AND TRUSTING —TRUSTING AND NOT FEARING

What time I am afraid, I will trust in thee (Psalm 56:3).
I will trust, and not be afraid (Isaiah 12:2).

I INTEND THIS EVENING to have two texts, though I shall not therefore have two sermons, and so keep you a double length of time. Our first text, which will suffice to begin with, is in the 56th Psalm, at the 3rd verse:—"*What time I am afraid, I will trust in thee.*"

David was one of the boldest of men. From his youth up, he was noted for his courage. As a youth he went, in simple confidence in God, and attacked the giant Goliath. Throughout life there was no man who seemed to be more at home in wars and battles, and less likely to be afraid. But yet this hero, this courageous man, says that he was sometimes afraid, and I suppose that there are none of us but must plead guilty to the impeachment that sometimes the brave spirit gives way, and that we tremble and are afraid. It is a disease for which the cure is here mentioned, "What time I am afraid, I will trust in thee; when my soul suffers from the palsy of fear, I will lay hold upon the strong one, and get strength from him, and so my fears shall all be cast out."

To be afraid is, in some cases, *a very childish thing*. We expect to see our little children sometimes frightened, and that they will not bear to be alone in the dark, but we are surely not afraid to be there. The more we are afraid, the more childish we become. Courage is manly, but to be afraid is to be like a child. It is not always so, however, for there are some great and sore dangers which may well make the very boldest man tremble.

To be afraid is always *a distressing thing* as well. The heart beats quickly, and the whole system seems to be

17

thrown out of order. There have been known cases of men who have had to endure severe terror for several hours, and their hair has all turned gray in a single night. No doubt, too, there have been diseases which have brought men to their graves, and which have been caused by fright. Fear is always distressing, and whether it be the fear of outward danger, or fear of inward sin, it is always a terrible thing to have to go mourning because of being afraid.

To be afraid, too, is always *a weakening thing*. The man who can keep calm in the midst of difficulty is better able to meet it. If he be at sea in a storm, if his mind be quiet, he is likely to steer his vessel safely through the danger, but if he be perturbed and cast down with agitated alarm, we can have but little confidence in him, for we know not where he may steer the ship. A man who is afraid often runs into worse dangers than those from which he seeks to escape. He plunges himself into the sea to escape from the river, and it is as though he fled from a lion, and a bear met him.

To be afraid, then, is generally a very mischievous thing, and though sometimes exceedingly excusable, yet full often is exceedingly dangerous also. David, however, here gives us the cure for fear, "What time I am afraid, I will trust in thee."

I shall not have time this evening to discuss all the fears and amazements which distress humanity, but there are four or five which we will mention, and which may comprehend the others:

Sometimes We Are Afraid of Temporal Troubles

If some of you have such a smooth path in life that you are untried in this respect, yet the great proportion of mankind have a hard fight to find bread to eat, and raiment wherewith they shall be clothed, and in the lives of the poor, especially, there must often be sad times when they are afraid lest they should not be able to provide things necessary, and should be brought to absolute starvation. Such a fear must very often afflict those who are in extreme poverty. And you, too, who are in business, in this age of competition, you are, no doubt, frequently afraid lest, by a failure in this direction or in that, you should not be able to meet your engagements, and the good ship of your business should drive upon the rocks. Such fears, I suppose, fall to the lot of all young tradesmen when they are starting in business life, and, peradventure, there are few older ones who have done longer and rougher work, are quite free from such times of anxious fear.

And, brethren, even if we have none of these troubles about what we shall eat and what we shall drink, yet we have our domestic troubles, that make us to be much alarmed. It is no small thing to see the child sick, or, worse still, to see your life's partner gradually fading away, and to know, as some do, that the case is beyond all medical skill, and that she, who is so dear, must be taken away.

And you wives, perhaps, are some of you dreading the hour when you may become widows, and your little children may be fatherless? You have often been afraid as you have looked forward to the calamity which seemed to overshadow you. God has not made this world to be a nest for us, and if we try to make it such for ourselves, he plants thorns in it, so that we may be compelled to mount and find our soul's true home somewhere else, in a higher and nobler sphere than this poor world can give.

Now, whenever we are tried with these temporal affairs, David tells us we are to trust in God. "What time I am afraid, I will trust in thee." I will just do this; after having done my best to earn my daily bread and to fight the battle of life, if I find I cannot do all I would, I will throw myself upon the promise of God, wherein he has said, "Thy bread shall be given thee, and thy water shall be sure." I will believe that my Heavenly Father, who feeds the ravens, will feed me, and that if he does not suffer even the gnats that dance in the sunbeam to perish for lack of sustenance, he will not suffer a soul that rests upon him to perish for lack of daily bread. Oh! it is a sweet thing, though, mayhap, you may some of you think it a hard thing—it is a sweet thing when God enables you to leave the morrow with him, and to depend upon your Father who is in heaven.

To the tradesman I speak, and all who have often to do business in great waters, who seem to go from water-spout to water-spout, and over whom all God's waves and billows seem to go—I believe you will find yourselves much stronger to do battle against these difficulties if it be your constant habit to commit all your cares to him who careth for you. It will all go wrong with us, even in smooth waters, if we do not have God to be the Pilot; and as to rough weather, we shall soon be a wreck if we forget him. I know of nothing more delightful to the believer than every morning to commit the day's troubles to God, and then go down into the world feeling, "Well, my Father knows it all," and then at night to commit the troubles of the day again into the great Father's hands, and to feel that he has said, "I will never leave thee, nor forsake thee." It is sweet sleeping when you can have a promise for the pillow at your head.

You know, perhaps, the good old story which is told of the woman on ship-board who was greatly afraid in a storm, but she saw her husband perfectly at peace, and she could not understand it. Her husband said he would tell her the reason, so snatching up a sword, he pointed it at her heart. She looked at it, but did not tremble. "Well," said he, "are you not afraid? The sword is sharp and I could kill you in a moment." "No," said she, "because it is in your hands!"

"Ah!" he replied, "and that is why I am not afraid, because the storm is in my Father's hands, and he loves me better than I love you."

A little child was at play in a lower room, and as he played away by himself, amusing himself, about every ten minutes he ran to the foot of the stairs and called out, "Mother, are you there?" and his mother answered, "Yes, I am here," and the little lad went back to his sport and fun, and was as happy as happy could be, until again it crossed his mind that his mother might have gone. So he ran to the stairs again and called, "Mother, are you there?" "All right," she said, and as soon as he heard her voice again, back he went once more to his play.

It is just so with us. In times of temporal trouble we go to the mercy-seat in prayer, and we say, "Father, art thou there? Is it thy hand that is troubling me? Is it thy Providence that has sent me this difficulty?" And as soon as you hear the voice which saith, "It is I," you are no longer afraid. Oh! happy are they who, when they are afraid in this way, trust in the Lord.

A second great fear, through which some of you have never passed, but through which all must pass who enter into heaven, is a:

Fear Concerning the Guilt of Past Sin

Do not tell me with regard to temporal troubles that they are sharp and bitter! Believe me, that trouble for sin is far more bitter and keen. Do you remember when God was pleased to awaken you from your long sleep, when you looked within, and saw that you were all defiled, and full of pollution, and all manner of evil? Do you recollect how the thoughts pierced you like poisoned arrows—"God requireth that which is pure"; "For every idle word that men shall speak, they shall give an account thereof at the day of judgment"? Do you recollect how it seemed as though hell flared up right before you where you stood, and it seemed as though there were a step only betwixt you and death?

The terrors of the Lord got hold upon you, and the very marrow of your bones seemed to freeze as you thought upon an angry God, and of how you, in your sins, without any preparation, could meet him! Oh! it is not so long ago with some of us but what we recollect being startled in our sleep under a sense of sin; and all day long the common joys of men were no joys to us, and though before we had been sprightly and cheerful like others, yet our mirth was now turned into mourning, and all our laughter into lamentation!

Perhaps some of you are passing through this state of mind now. You are conscious now of your old sins: the sins of your youth are coming up before your remembrance. Now, if so, listen to what David says, "What time I am afraid, I will trust in thee."

Beloved! if you would ever get rid of the fear of your past sins, remember that the Lord Jesus Christ came into the world to suffer for the sins of all who will trust him. All the sins of all his people were reckoned as upon him, and all that they should have suffered on account of those sins Jesus Christ suffered in their stead. The mighty debt, too huge for us to calculate, was all laid upon him, and he paid it to the farthing. He was sued and summoned at the court of the eternal justice, for the sins of his people were reckoned as upon him, and all that they should have rendered with hands and feet, and brow and side, he discharged: the whole tremendous debt that was due to God, the debt caused by the sins of all his people were paid by him.

Now, it is a blessed thing when sin burdens us to fly away to Christ, and stand in spirit beneath the cross, and feel that under that crimson canopy no flash of divine penalty shall ever fall upon us. "Smite me! Great God? Thou canst not, for hast thou not smitten the redeeming Christ on my account? Is it not recorded that for those who trust him, thy Son is both surety and substitute? How, then, canst thou first sue the Substitute, and then afterwards sue the person, for whom the Substitute stood?"

Faith thus clings to the cross, and feels, nay! knows, that all is safe. I would God that some of you who are lamenting over the burden of your sins, and are pressed down by it, would look to the Son of God pouring out his life, and would trust him, for then your sins would be gone in a moment. Only look on Jesus, and though you had committed all the sins that are committable by mortal man, yet Jesus Christ can put them all away. If every form of iniquity were heaped upon you, till you were dyed through and through with it, like the scarlet that has been lying long a-soak in the dye, yet let the crimson blood of Jesus come into contact with your crimson sins, and they:

> "Shall vanish ill away,
> Though foul as hell before;
> Shall be dissolved beneath the sea,
> And shall be found no more."

Now, I know it is very easy when we do not feel our sins to trust in Christ, but the business of faith is to trust in Christ when you *do* feel your sins. Brethren, it would be cheap faith to take Christ as the saints' Savior, but it is the faith of God's elect to take him as the sinner's Savior. When I can see marks of grace in myself, to trust Christ is easy; but when I see no marks of anything good, but every mark of everything that is evil, and then come and cast myself upon him, and believe that he can save me, even me, and rest myself upon him—this is the faith which honors Christ and which will save us. May you have it, and such time as you are afraid of sin, may you trust in Christ. A third fear, which is remarkably common, is a:

Fear Lest We Should Be Deceived

Among the best and most careful of believers this fear intrudes itself. "Lest, after having preached to others, I myself should be a castaway," Paul said. Lest, after having been united to the church, I should prove to be a dead member, and so be cut out of the living vine. All these fears have I met with. One has said, "I fear I was never chosen of God." Another has said, "I fear I never was effectually called." And yet a third has said, "I fear I never possessed the repentance that needeth not to be repented of."

Still others have confessed, "I am afraid my faith is not the faith of God's elect." Very frequently have I heard this, "I am afraid I am a hypocrite," which is one of the strangest fears in all the world, for nobody who was a hypocrite was ever afraid of it. It is the hypocrite who goes on peacefully, without fear, confident where there is no ground for confidence. But these fears abound, and in some respects, they are healthy. Better go to heaven *doubting*, than to hell *presuming*. Better to enter into life halt and maimed, than, having two eyes and hands, and feet, to be cast into the destroying fire. We cannot say too much in praise of assurance, and we cannot speak too much against presumption. Dread that! shun it with all your might.

But when you and I are besieged by these doubts and fears—and I very often am—as to whether we are the children of God or not, what is the best thing for us to do?

"What time I am afraid, I will trust in thee." This is the shortcut with the devil. This is the way to cut off his head more readily than anyhow else. Go straight away to Christ. Do not stop to argue with Satan. He is a crafty old liar, and he will be sure to defeat you if it comes to argument between you. Say to him, "Satan, if I be deceived, if all I have ever known up till now has been only head-knowledge, if I am nothing but a mere hypocrite, yet now:

"Black, I to the fountain fly;
Wash me, Savior, or I die."

It is a blessed thing to begin again; to be always beginning, and yet always going on, for no man ever goes on to perfection who forgets his first love, his first faith, and forgets to walk in Christ Jesus as he walked in him at the first.

Beloved, whatever may be the doubt that comes to you at this moment, I beseech you recollect it is still, "Him that cometh unto me I will in no wise cast out." If you have been a backslider, weep over it; if you have been a great sinner, be sorry for it, but still remember, "All manner of sin and of blasphemy shall be forgiven unto men," and "Where sin abounded, grace doth much more abound." The gospel's voice still is, "Return, ye backsliding children, for I am married unto you, saith the Lord." "Come, now, let us reason together; though your sins be as scarlet, they shall be as wool; though they be red like crimson, they shall be whiter than snow." Come, come, come, thou doubting one; trembling and broken to pieces; come again, a guilty, weak, and helpless worm, and cast yourself into Jesus' arms.

But we cannot tarry upon that. A fourth fear, which is frequent enough to cause Christians much distress, is:

A Fear That We Shall Not Hold On, and Hold Out, to the End

Many thousands of God's saints are quite unnecessarily troubled with this. Remember, that where God begins to work, he does not ask us to finish it. He always completes his own work. If you have begun the work of salvation, you will have to carry it on, but if God has begun the good work in you, he will carry it on, and bring to perfection of completeness in "the day of Christ." Yet there are thousands who say, "Should I be tempted, I might fall: working as I do with so many others, none of whom, perhaps, turn aside and prove like one of them." It is very proper that you should have that fear, very proper that you should be distressed at it.

"What anguish has that question stirred, If I should also go!"

But, dearly beloved, what time you are afraid, do not say, "I shall be able to hold out"; do not trust in yourselves, or you will trust to a broken reed, but what time you are afraid, renew your trust in Christ. Go with the temptation which you now experience, and which you expect to recur tomorrow, to the Lord, and he will, with the temptation, show the way of escape out of it.

I remember a miner who had been a sad, drunken man, and a great blasphemer, but he was converted among the Methodists, and a right earnest man he was, but he seemed to have been a man of strong passions, and on one occasion he was praying, and he prayed that sooner than that he might ever go back to his old sins, if God foresaw that he would not be able to bear up under temptation, he would take him to heaven at once, and while he was praying the prayer in the prayer-meeting he fell dead. God had answered him.

Now, if you are to be tried in the order of Providence in a way that you cannot bear, and there is no other way of escape for you, God will take you clear away to where no temptation shall ever come near you. What time you are afraid, put your trust in him, and all will be well.

The last fear I have to mention, and then I shall have done with my first text, is this:

The Fear of Death

There are some "who, through fear of death, are all their lifetime subject to bondage"; but Christ came to deliver such, and where Christ works he delivers us from that fear. Beloved, are you ever afraid of death? You are, perhaps, when you feel very sick, when you are very ill and low-spirited. You begin to look forward, and you say, "I have run with the footmen and they have wearied me; what shall I do when I have to contend with the rider on the pale horse? My trials have been so great that I have scarcely found faith enough to bear them; what shall I do in the last great trial of the swellings of Jordan?"

Now, what ought you to do at what time you are afraid of dying, but to say, with David, "What time I am afraid, I will trust in thee"? Oh! fear not to die! If you are in Christ, death is nothing. "But the pain, the dying struggle," you say. Oh! there is no pain in death. It is the life that is full of pain. Death! What is it? Well, it is but a pin's prick, and then it is over. "Many lie a-dying for weeks or months together," say some. Nay! say they live, for 'tis living that makes them full of pain and anguish, but death ends all that. Death is just the passing through the narrow stream that is the entrance in the fields where:—

"Everlasting spring abides, and never-withering flowers."

To be afraid to die must be because we do not understand it, for if believers know that to die is but to enter into the arms of Jesus Christ, surely they will be able to sing bravely with one good old saint:

> "Since Jesus is mine, I'll not fear undressing,
> But gladly put off this garment of clay.
> To die in the Lord is a covenant blessing,
> Since Jesus to glory, through death, led the way."

What time you are afraid of dying, trust in the living Savior, for in him are life and immortality. Recollect:

> "Jesus can make our dying bed
> Feel soft as downy pillows are,
> Whilst on his breast we lean our head,
> And breathe our life out softly there."

He will keep you where you shall sing:—

> "Oh! if my Lord would come and meet,
> My soul would stretch her wings in haste;

Fly fearless through death's iron gate,
Nor fear the terror as she passed."

You shall fear no fear, and know no evil, because he shall be with you, and you shall find that his rod and his staff do comfort you.

Now, brethren, I have taken you far, like a guide conducting a number of travelers up the first road on a mountain, and I think we have gathered something even there, but now I want you to go up higher still. I feel as if, in handling this text, we have been traveling third class to heaven, but now I want you to get into the first class. Hitherto we have been going in a sort of parliamentary train, which will get to heaven safe enough, but I want you now to take the express.

My second text will let you know what I mean. It is in the twelfth chapter of Isaiah and the second verse: "*I will trust and not be afraid.*"

This is several stages beyond the first text. David says, "What time I am afraid, I will trust in thee." Isaiah says, "I will trust and not be afraid," which is far better. When David is afraid he trusts in God, but Isaiah trusts in God first, and then he is not afraid at all. I told you in the first case that there was a disease, and that faith was the remedy, but you know prevention is always better than cure. I have heard of a man who had the ague, and he was thankful to have a medicine which helped him through it; but his neighbor said he should not be very thankful for that, for he had a remedy which prevented him from ever having the malady.

So with you who are doubting and fearing: it is a good thing that faith can bear you through it, but how much better it will be if you get a faith that does not have these doubts, that lives above these fears and troubles.

See! There are two vessels yonder, and a storm is coming on. I see a great hurrying and scurrying on the deck of one. What are they doing? They have a great anchor, and they are throwing it out. The storm is coming, and they want to get a good hold, for fear lest they should be driven on the shore.

But on the deck of the other vessel, I see no bustle at

all. There is the watch pacing up and down as leisurely as possible. Why are they not in a panic? "Ahoy there! Ahoy! What makes you so calm and assured? Have you got out your anchor? See you! Your comrades in the other vessel, how busy they are!" "Oh!" says the watch, "but we had our anchor out a long while ago, before the storm came on, and therefore we have no need to trouble now, and hurry to throw it out."

Now, you who are full of doubts, and fears, and troubles, you know the way to be safe is to throw out the anchor of faith, but it would be better still if you had the anchor of faith out already, so that you could trust in God, and not be afraid at all.

Let us take the fears which we have already mentioned over again. Faith saves from:

The Fear of Temporal Trouble

The man who fully trusts in God is not afraid of temporal trouble. You have read, perhaps, the life of Bernard Palissy, the famous potter. He was confined for many years on account of his religion, and he was only permitted to live at all because he was such a skillful workman that they did not like to put him to death.

King Henry the Third of France said to him one day, "Bernard, I shall be obliged to give you up to the enemies to be burned, unless you change your religion." Bernard replied, "Your Majesty, I have often heard you say you pity me, but believe me I greatly pity you, though I am no king but only a poor humble potter, but there is no man living who could compel me to do what I believe to be wrong; and yet you say you will be compelled; those are kingly words for you to utter!" And he could say this to the king, in whose hands his life was!

Bernard was a very poor man. As I have told you, he used to earn his bread by making pottery, and he used to say in his poverty that he was a very rich man, for he had two things, he had heaven and earth, and then he would take up a handful of the clay by which he earned his living. Happy man! Though often brought to the depths of poverty, he could say, "I will trust and not be afraid."

Take as another example, Martin Luther. They came to Martin one day, and they said, "Martin, it is all over with the Reformation cause now, for the Emperor of Germany has sworn a solemn oath to help the Pope." "I do not care a snap of my finger for both of them," said he, "nor for all the devils in hell! This is God's work, and God's work can stand against both emperors and popes."

There was a man who trusted, really, intensely, and because of this he was not afraid. Is not that much better than being afraid, and then having to trust to banish the fear? Now, God is with me, and come what may:

> "Should earth against my soul engage,
> And hellish darts be hurled;
> Now I can smile at Satan's rage,
> And face a frowning world.
> "Let cares like a wild deluge come,
> And storms of sorrow fall:
> I shall in safety reach my home,
> My God, my heaven, my all."

Oh! if we can all get to this brave assurance of faith, happy shall we be in the midst of the worst trouble. Faith also saves from the:

Fear Concerning Past Sin

He is in a blessed state who is delivered from such fear, because he who is not is not afraid. One of you knows a man, perhaps, who has gotten into debt, and who owed a great deal. But some little time ago a friend paid all his debts for him, and he has the receipt. Now, when he walks the streets, is this man afraid of the sheriff's officer? Does he fear that he shall be arrested? Why, no; he knows he shall not, because he has the receipt about him. Every man who trusts Christ perceives his own sin, but he also perceives that Christ paid for all his sin. He that believeth hath the witness of his pardon in himself, which he carries about him as a receipt, and which eases his conscience and prevents his fears. Oh! if you can but know that Christ died for you; if you can but rest alone in him so as to know that he is yours, then all the sins that you have ever committed, though you lament them, shall never cause you a moment's uneasiness, for they are drowned beneath the Red Sea of the Savior's blood, and therefore may you say, "I will trust and not be afraid." As to that third fear which I mentioned—the fear lest we should be hypocrites, or:

Lest the Work of Grace Should Not Be Ripened in Our Hearts

There is one way of getting rid of that fear entirely. If you take a coin across the counter, you may not know whether it is a good one; you may have some doubts about it. But if you get it straight from the Mint, I do not suppose you will have any suspicion of it at all. So when a man asks, "Is my faith right? Is my religion right?" If he can say, "I got it straight from the throne of God by trusting in the blood of Jesus Christ"—then he will know that he received it from headquarters, and there can be no mistake about it. A Christian has no right to be always saying:

"Do I love the Lord or no?
Am I his, or am I not?"

He may be compelled to say it sometimes, but it is far better for him to come just as he is, and throw himself at the foot of the cross, and say, "Savior, thou hast promised to save those who believe! I do believe, therefore thou hast saved me." I know some think this is presumption, but surely it is worse than presumption not to believe God, and it is true humility to take God at his word, and to believe him.

I think I once illustrated this truth in this place in this way. A good mother has two children. Christmas is drawing near, and she says to one of them, "Now, John, I shall take you out on Christmas Day to such a place, and give you a great treat." She promises the same to William. Now, Master John says to himself, "Well, I do not know: I do not know whether my mother can afford it: or perhaps I do not deserve it: I hardly think she will take me: it will be presumption in me to believe that she will."

But as for little Master William, he is no sooner told

that he is to go out on Christmas Day than he claps his hands, and begins to skip, and tells all his playmates tomorrow that his mother is going to take him out on Christmas Day: he is quite sure of it. They begin to ask him, "How do you know?" "Why," he says, "mother said so." Perhaps they mention some things that make it look rather unlikely. "Oh! but," he says, "my mother never tells lies, and she told me she would take me, and I know she will."

Now, which of those children do you think, is most to be commended—the bigger boy, who raised difficulties and suspected his mother's word? Why, he is a proud little fellow, who deserves to go without the pleasure; but as for the little brother William, who takes his mother at her word—I do not call him proud. I consider him truly humble, and he is the child who really deserves the mother's fondest love. Now, deal with God as you would have your children deal with you. If he says he will save you if you trust him, then if you do trust him, why, he will save you. If he is a true God, he cannot destroy the soul that trusts in Christ. Unless this Bible is one great lie from beginning to end the soul that trusts in Christ must be saved. If God be true, every soul that trusts in Jesus must be safe at the last. Whatever he may be, and whoever he may be, if he trusts his soul with Christ, and with Christ alone, cast away he cannot be, unless the promise of God can be of no effect. "I will trust and not be afraid."

So, brethren, it will be with other fears—time fails us to mention them—whatever they may be. May you get into such a blessed state of confidence in the love of God, in the love of Christ's heart, in the power of Christ's arm, in the prevalence of Christ's plea, that at all times you may trust in him, and in nothing whatever be afraid.

God bring us all up to this second platform, and give us grace to keep there, and happy shall you be, and have a foretaste of heaven upon earth. Amen.

Love and Fear

Alexander Maclaren (1826-1910) was one of Great Britain's most famous preachers. While pastoring the Union Chapel, Manchester (1858-1903), he became known as "the prince of expository preachers." Rarely active in denominational or civic affairs, Maclaren invested his time studying the Word in the original and sharing its truths with others in sermons that are still models of effective expository preaching. He published a number of books of sermons and climaxed his ministry by publishing his monumental *Expositions of Holy Scripture*. This message is taken from *Triumphant Certainties and Other Sermons*, published by Funk and Wagnalls Company (1902).

Alexander Maclaren

3

LOVE AND FEAR

There is no fear in love, but perfect love casteth out fear: because fear hath torment. He that feareth is not made perfect in love (1 John 4:18).

JOHN HAS BEEN SPEAKING of boldness, and that naturally suggests its opposite—fear. He has been saying that perfect love produces courage in the day of judgment, because it produces likeness to Christ, who is the Judge. In my text he explains and enlarges that statement. For there is another way in which love produces boldness, and that is by casting out fear. These two are mutually exclusive. The entrance of the one is for the other a notice to quit. We cannot both love and fear the same person or thing, and where love comes in, the darker form slips out at the door; and where Love comes in, it brings hand in hand with itself Courage with her radiant face. But boldness is the companion of love, only when love is perfect. For, inconsistent as the two emotions are, love, in its earlier stages and lower degrees, is often perturbed and dashed by apprehension and dread.

Now John is speaking about the two emotions in themselves, irrespective, so far as his language goes, of the objects to which they are directed. What he is saying is true about love and fear, whatever or whosoever may be loved or dreaded. But the context suggests the application in his mind, for it is "boldness before him" about which he has been speaking; and so it is love and fear directed towards God which are meant in my text. The experience of hosts of professing Christians is only too forcible a comment upon the possibility of a partial Love lodging in the heart side by side with a fellow-lodger, Fear, whom it ought to have expelled. So there are three things here that I wish to notice—the empire of fear, the mission of fear, and the expulsion of fear.

The Empire of Fear

Fear is a shrinking apprehension of evil as befalling us, from the person or thing which we dread. My text brings us face to face with the solemn thought that there are conditions of human nature, in which the God who ought to be our dearest joy and most ardent desire becomes our ghastliest dread. The root of such an unnatural perversion of all that a creature ought to feel towards its loving Creator lies in the simple consciousness of discordance between God and man, which is the shadow cast over the heart by the fact of sin. God is righteous; God righteously administers His universe. God enters into relations of approval or disapproval with His responsible creature. Therefore there lies, dormant for the most part, but present in every heart, and active in the measure in which that heart is informed as to itself, the slumbering cold dread that between it and God things are *not* as they ought to be.

I believe, for my part, that such a dumb, dim consciousness of discord attaches to all men, though it is often smothered, often ignored, and often denied. But there it is; the snake hibernates, but it is coiled in the heart all the same; and warmth will awake it. Then it lifts its crested head, and shoots out its forked tongue, and venom passes into the veins. A dread of God is the ghastliest thing in the world, the most unnatural, but universal, unless expelled by perfect love.

Arising from that discomforting consciousness of discord there come, likewise, other forms and objects of dread. For if I am out of harmony with Him, what will be my fate in the midst of a universe administered by Him, and in which all are His servants? Oh! I sometimes wonder how it is that godless men front the facts of human life, and do not go mad. For here are we, naked, feeble, alone, plunged into a whirlpool, from the awful vortices of which we cannot extricate ourselves. There foam and swirl all manner of evils, some of them certain, some of them probable, any of them possible, since we are at discord with Him who wields all the forces of the universe, and wields them all with a righteous hand. "The stars in their courses fight against" the man who does not fight for God.

Whilst all things serve the soul that serves Him, all are embattled against the man that is against, or not for, God and His will.

Then there arises up another object of dread, which, in like manner, derives all its power to terrify and to hurt from the fact of our discordance with God; and that is "the shadow feared of man," that stands shrouded by the path, and waits for each of us.

God; God's universe; God's messenger, Death—these are facts with which we stand in relation, and if our relations with Him are out of gear, then He and all of these are legitimate objects of dread to us.

But now there is something else that casts out fear than perfect love, and that is—perfect levity. For it is the explanation of the fact that so many of us know nothing of this fear of which I speak, and fancy that I am exaggerating, or putting forward false views. There is a type of man, and I have no doubt there are some of its representatives among my hearers, who are below both fear and love as directed towards God; for they never think about Him, or trouble their heads concerning either Him or their relations to Him or anything that flows therefrom. It is a strange faculty that we all have, of forgetting unwelcome thoughts and shutting our eyes to the things that we do not want to see, like Nelson when he put the telescope to his blind eye at Copenhagen, because he would not obey the signal of recall. But surely it is an ignoble thing that men should ignore or shuffle out of sight with inconsiderateness the real facts of their condition, like boys whistling in a churchyard to keep their spirits up, and saying "Who's afraid?" just because they are so very much afraid. Ah! dear friends, do not rest until you face the facts, and having faced them, have found the way to reverse them. Surely, surely it is not worthy of men, to turn away from anything so certain as that between a sin-loving man and God there must exist such a relation as will bring evil and sorrow to that man, as surely as God is and he is. I beseech you, take to heart these things, and do not turn away from them with a shake of your shoulders, and say, "He is preaching the narrow, old-fashioned doctrine of a religion of fear." No! I am not. But I am preaching this plain fact, that a man who is in discord with God has reason to be afraid, and I come to you with the old exhortation of the prophet, "Be troubled, ye careless ones." For there is nothing more ignoble or irrational than security which is only made possible by covering over unwelcome facts. "Be troubled"; and let the trouble lead you to the Refuge.

That brings me to the second point—viz.,

The Mission of Fear

John uses a rare word in my text when he says "fear hath torment." "Torment" does not convey the whole idea of the word. It means suffering, but suffering for a purpose; suffering which is correction; suffering which is disciplinary; suffering which is intended to lead to something beyond itself. Fear, the apprehensions of personal evil, has the same function in the moral world as pain has in the physical. It is a symptom of disease, and is intended to bid us look for the remedy and the Physician. What is an alarm bell for, but to rouse the sleepers, and to hurry them to the refuge? And so this wholesome, manly dread of the certain issue of discord with God is meant to do for us what the angels did for Lot—to lay a mercifully violent hand on the shoulder of the sleeper, and shake him into aroused wakefulness, and hasten him out of Sodom, before the fire bursts through the ground, and is met by the fire from above. The intention of fear is to lead to that which shall annihilate it by taking away its cause.

There is nothing more ridiculous, nothing more likely to destroy a man, than the indulgence in an idle fear which does nothing to prevent its own fulfillment. Horses in a burning stable are so paralyzed by dread that they cannot stir, and get burnt to death. And for a man to be afraid—as everyone ought to be who is conscious of unforgiven sin—for a man to be afraid and there an end, is absolute insanity. I fear; then what do I do? Nothing. That is true about hosts of us.

What ought I to do? Let the dread direct me to its source, my own sinfulness. Let the discovery of my own sinfulness direct me to its remedy, the righteousness and the Cross of Jesus Christ. He, and He alone, can deal with the disturbing element in my relation to God. He can "deliver me from my enemies, for they are too strong for me." It is Christ and His work, Christ and His sacrifice, Christ and His indwelling Spirit that will grapple with and overcome sin and all its consequences, in any man and in every man—taking away its penalty, lightening the heart of the burden of its guilt, delivering from its love and dominion. All three of these things are the barbs of the arrows with which fear riddles heart and conscience. So my fear should proclaim to me the merciful "name that is above every name," and drive me as well as draw me to Christ, the Conqueror of sin, and the Antagonist of all dread.

Brethren, I said I was not preaching the religion of Fear. But I think we shall scarcely understand the religion of Love unless we recognize that dread is a legitimate part of an unforgiven man's attitude towards God. My fear should be to me like the misshapen guide that may lead me to the fortress where I shall be safe. Oh! do not tamper with the wholesome sense of dread. Do not let it lie, generally sleeping, and now and then waking in your hearts, and bringing about nothing. Sailors that crash on with all sails set, whilst the barometer is rapidly falling, and boding clouds are on the horizon, and the line of the approaching gale is ruffling the sea yonder, have themselves to blame if they founder. Look to the falling barometer, and make ready for the coming storm, and remember that the mission of fear is to lead you to the Christ who will take it away.

Lastly, let us look at . . .

The Expulsion of Fear

My text points out the natural antagonism, and mutual exclusiveness, of these two emotions. If I go to Jesus Christ as a sinful man, and get His love bestowed upon me, then, as the next verse to my text says, my love springs in response to His to me, and in the measure in which that love rises in my heart will it frustrate its antagonistic dread.

As I said, you cannot love and fear the same person, unless the love is of a very rudimentary and imperfect character. But, just as when you pour pure water into a bladder, the poisonous gases that it may have contained will be driven out before it, so when love comes in, dread goes out. The river, turned into the foulness of the heart, will sweep out all the filth and leave everything clean. The black, greasy smoke-wreath, touched by the fire of Christ's love, will flash out into ruddy flames, like that which has kindled them; and Christ's love will kindle in your hearts, if you accept it and apprehend it aright, a love which shall burn up and turn into fuel for itself the now useless dread.

But, brethren, remember that it is *"perfect* love" which "casts out fear."

Inconsistent as the two emotions are in themselves in practice, they may be united, by reason of the imperfection of the nobler. And in the Christian life they are united with terrible frequency. There are many professing Christians who live all their days with a burden of shivering dread upon their shoulders, and an icy cold fear in their hearts, just because they have not got close enough to Jesus Christ, nor kept their hearts with sufficient steadfastness under the quickening influences of His love, to have shaken off their dread as a sick man's distempered fancies.

A little love has not mass enough in it to drive out thick, clustering fears. There are hundreds of professing Christians who know very little indeed of that joyous love of God which swallows up and makes impossible all dread, who, because they have not a loving present consciousness of a loving Father's loving will, tremble when they confront in imagination, and still more when they meet in reality, the evils that must come. They cannot face the thought of death with anything but shrinking apprehension. There is far too much of the old leaven of selfish dread left in the experiences of many Christians. "I feared thee, because thou wert an austere man, and so, because I was afraid, I went and hid my talent, and did nothing for thee" is a transcript of the experience of far too many of us. The one way to get deliverance is to go to Jesus Christ and keep close by Him.

And my last word to you is, see that you resort only to the sane, sound way of getting rid of the wholesome, rational dread of which I have been speaking. You can ignore it; and buy immunity at the price of leaving in full operation the *causes* of your dread—and that is stupid. There is only one wise thing to do, and that is, to make sure work of getting rid of the occasion of dread, which is the fact of sin. Take all your sin to Jesus Christ; He will—and He only can—deal with it. He will lay His hand on you, as He did of old, with the characteristic word that was so often upon His lips, and which He alone is competent to speak in its deepest meaning, "Fear not, it is I," and He will give you the courage that He commands.

"God hath not given us the spirit of fear, but of power, and love, and of a sound mind." "Ye have not received the spirit of bondage again to fear, but ye have received the spirit of adoption, whereby we cry Abba, Father," and cling to Him, as a child who knows his father's heart too well to be afraid of anything in his father, or of anything that his father's hand can send.

Fear

Clarence Edward Noble Macartney (1879-1957)
ministered in Paterson, New Jersey, and Philadelphia,
Pennsylvania, before assuming the influential pastorate
of First Presbyterian Church, Pittsburgh, where he
ministered for twenty-seven years. His preaching especially
attracted men, not only to the Sunday services but also to
his popular Tuesday noon luncheons. He was gifted in
dealing with Bible biographies, and, in this respect, has
well been called "the American Alexander Whyte." Much
of his preaching was topical-textual, but it was always
biblical, doctrinal and practical. Perhaps his most famous
sermon is "Come Before Winter." The sermon I have
selected is taken from *You Can Conquer*, published in 1954
by Abingdon Press, New York and Nashville.

Clarence Edward Noble Macartney

4

FEAR

> I sought the Lord, and he heard me, and delivered me from all my fears (Psalm 34:4).

FEAR IS MAN'S ENEMY number one. It was the first enemy which attacked man. When at the beginning man broke the commandment of God and then heard the voice of God walking in the garden he was afraid and hid himself among the trees of the garden. Paul calls death the "last enemy," and since man fears death, fear is, therefore, man's first and last enemy.

How many kinds of fear there are! If one could take a station in front of a church in a large city and have the power to look into the hearts and minds of the thousands who pass by every day, what a multitude of fears would be revealed: fear for the body, fear of sickness, fear for the mind, fear of poverty, fear of losing the job, fear of criticism, fear of temptation, fear of the consequences of wrongdoing, fear of loneliness, fear of old age, fear of the past, fear of things present and things to come, and fear of the last enemy, which is death. Beyond these standard fears, men are haunted with strange fears, such as the fear of being buried alive. Samuel Johnson, the great lexicographer, was afraid to pass a post without touching it. Some fear to pass under a ladder on the street or to sit down at a table when the number of people to be seated is thirteen.

A gifted professor of the University of Wisconsin, William Ellery Leonard, for thirty-five years was a prisoner of a strange fear and never went further away from his house than five blocks. He attributed this fear to a fright he had when he was three years old.

It is not strange then that the Bible has so much to say upon the subject of fear. Almost more frequently than anything else it says, "Fear not," "Be not afraid," "Be of good courage," "Be of good cheer," "Let not your heart be troubled." Like the sound of a trumpet this note echoes through the book of Psalms, and we hear its echo in the words of the text—"I sought the Lord, and he heard me, and delivered me from all my fears."

Many of the fears which trouble men are altogether imaginary and illusory. A man traveling in a lonely region was terrified when he saw in the distance, coming toward him, what he thought was a monster. When it came a little closer, he saw that it was not a monster, but a man; and when it came still closer, he saw that the man was his own brother.

George Herbert, the gifted English poet, had a saying about ghosts. If you see a ghost at night, the thing to do is to go up to speak to it, and you will find that the ghost is nothing more than a sheet hung out to dry!

A young black boy in the South who was afraid to go up into the loft of his cabin to sleep lest he should see a ghost was told "there are no ghosts." His answer was, "I'm not afraid of the ghosts that are, but of the ghosts that ain't."

Alexander the Great, on a campaign with his army from Macedonia to India, rode a beautiful black horse called Bucephalus. The horse had been brought by horse traders to the court of Philip, Alexander's father, for use in his calvary; but he seemed to be so vicious, plunging and kicking at everyone who came near him, that the king's horseman was about to reject him. Alexander was greatly taken with the animal and asked permission of his father to ride him. When Philip gave his consent, Alexander, who had noted that the horse was frightened by his shadow, took him by the bridle and turned his head into the sun. Then he leaped to his back and galloped up and down before the king.

The thing which frightens people is often only a shadow. They are afraid where no fear is. When the disciples saw Jesus walking over the sea that night of the storm on the Sea of Galilee, they were terrified and thought he was a ghost. But he was not a ghost, but their friend and master; and soon they heard his voice saying, "It is I; be not afraid." There is truth in that verse of the old hymn:

Ye fearful saints, fresh courage take;
The clouds ye so much dread
Are big with mercy, and shall break
In blessings on your head.

Fear for the Body

Let us look now at some of the common fears which
assail man—first of all, is fear for the body, the fear of
disease. Here the attitude of mind counts for a great deal.
A man who was in good health, going down the street to
his business, was accosted by a friend who told him he
thought he was not looking well. A little further along,
another met him and said the same thing. This frightened
him so that he went home and took to his bed.

The testimony of physicians and psychiatrists is that a
great many ailments of the body have no reality outside
the mind of the one who thinks he is sick, and that what
is needed is not the physician's medicine, but the medicine
of faith. There are, however, plenty of real ailments of the
body. The hospitals are filled with people who are really
sick. yet fear makes their illness worse and the cure of it
more difficult. The very mention of cancer, tuberculosis,
and heart disease—three great killers—fills many with
dread, a dread which keeps many who are afflicted with
such a disease from consulting a physician in time.

A Philadelphia physician said to me of a woman upon
whom I called when she was dying of cancer, that had she
come to him in time, he could have saved her life. But
fear held her back.

There is a legend of a peasant who, driving into a city
in Europe, was hailed by an aged woman who asked him
to take her up into his wagon and drive her into the town
with him. Looking at her as they drove along, the peasant
became alarmed and asked who she was. She told him
that she was the plague, cholera. The peasant then ordered
her out of his cart, but she assured him that in the city
she would kill only ten persons. As proof of her pledge she
handed him a dagger and told him that if she slew more
than ten, he was to take the dagger and slay her.

After they reached the city, more than a hundred

perished with the plague. The angry peasant, meeting the woman on the street, drew his dagger and was about to slay her. But she lifted her hand and told him that she had kept her word. "I killed only ten. Fear killed the rest."

The Christian believer must always remember that even when victory over sickness is impossible, victory *in* sickness is always possible. The great example of that is the apostle Paul, who had that grievous thorn in the flesh for which he besought the Lord so earnestly that it might depart from him. His request was not granted. But the Lord said to him, "My grace is sufficient for thee: for my strength is made perfect in weakness." In every sickness Christ is ready to give you and me the same promise, so that we too can say with Paul, "When I am weak, then am I strong."

Fear of Poverty

The fear of poverty, the loss of money, is one of the most ignoble of fears. I have come across wealthy men, who, toward the end of their lives, were obsessed with the fear of the loss of their fortune. That was because their money possessed them, rather than they possessing their money.

There are a number of considerations which guard against this fear of the loss of money. One is that, eventually, all of us will lose our money. In 1825 at the height of his fame when he was living at Abbotsford, his "romance in stone," Sir Walter Scott's printing house failed. In his diary for that period is this entry: "Naked we entered the world and naked we leave it; blessed be the name of the Lord. . . . I have walked my last in the domains I have planted—sat the last time in the halls I have built. But death would have taken them from me if misfortune had spared them."

How often we read in an obituary notice that a person has left so many thousands, or so many millions, of dollars. How true is that word "left." No matter how small or large his fortune, no man can take it with him. The great Moslem conqueror, Saladin, was buried with his hands protruding from his coffin to tell men that his hands were empty when he came into the world and empty also when he left. When Alexander the Great came back to Persepolis after his incredible conquests in India, he brought with him an Indian sage, Kalynas. As they stood together at the tomb of Karush, the founder of the Persian empire, Kalynas said to Alexander, "You have troubled much of the earth; but you own no more of it than that which will cover your body when you die."

That is true of us all. Job said, "Naked came I out of my mother's womb, and naked shall I return thither: the Lord gave, and the Lord hath taken away; blessed be the name of the Lord." And the apostle Paul said, "Godliness with contentment is great gain. For we brought nothing into this world, and it is certain we can carry nothing out." Nothing is more certain than that.

Another consideration which helps men master and conquer the fear of the loss of money is the things which money cannot do and cannot buy. It cannot buy health or a good conscience, or affection, or happiness. It has been well defined as that something which buys everything but happiness, and takes a man everywhere but heaven.

Fear of Old Age

Another common fear is the fear of old age. If we live long enough, old age is inevitable, and no one can deny the fact that great and strange are the changes wrought by time and age. Recently, I read the autobiography of a well-known woman on the Pacific coast, a woman who is now in her nineties. There was a picture of her as a young woman in college, then as a middle-aged woman, and then one of her in great age. As I looked at these pictures, I thought to myself, "How strange are the changes wrought by age!"

Men fear old age because of its failing strength. They fear it because of the dependence upon others which it brings. Jesus said to Peter, "When thou wast young, thou girdedst thyself, and walkedst whither thou wouldest: but when thou shalt be old, . . . another shall gird thee, and carry thee whither thou wouldest not." He was speaking of the violent martyr's death that Peter was to die in his old age. But how true a description of old age that phrase is, "Another shall gird thee." Men fear old age because of its fading enthusiasms. The expectation of youth is gone, and with the passing of that expectation, hope. In his old age Joseph Jefferson, the famous actor, spent a great deal of time in his garden. When asked why, he said that with the coming of old age many of the hopes and expectations of life faded, but when he planted things in his garden, he could at least look forward to their flowering and fruition.

Again, men fear old age because of its loneliness. To live is to outlive; in old age men find that their company has gone before. There is still another reason why men fear old age, and that is because, in the nature of things, old age is the anteroom to death.

What can we say, then, about this fear of old age? One is that old age is inevitable and appointed. It is as natural as infancy, or childhood, or middle life. In spite of the miracle drugs and the secrets of the beauty parlors, it is impossible to fend off old age. Therefore, do not quarrel with the inevitable.

A cheerful attitude of mind counts for much. There is a saying that we are as old as we feel. That is only a half truth. The whole truth is that we are as old as we are.

But think of the achievements of old age! Moses was ninety years old before he began his great work as a leader and deliverer of Israel. The British prime minister, Winston Churchill, was still a powerful voice and figure at almost eighty. Gladstone became prime minister for the fourth time at eighty-three and completed his translation of Horace at eighty-five. Michelangelo's greatest painting, "The Fresco of the Last Judgment," in the Sistine Chapel at Rome, was completed when he was almost seventy. On the threshold of his ninetieth year he was the chief architect of the Church of St. Peter's, the magnificent dome of which is his noblest monument. When he was eighty-seven, Titian finished for Philip the Second his "Last Supper," which you can see in Spain's vast Excorial. When he was almost a hundred, he was still producing paintings of great beauty and merit. In the words of Tennyson's "Ulysses":

Old age hath yet his honor and his toil;
Death closes all: but something ere the end,
Some work of noble note, may yet be done.

... And though

We are not now that strength which in old days
Moved earth and heaven, that which we are, we
are,—

One equal temper of heroic hearts,
Made weak by time and fate, but strong in will
To strive, to seek, to find, and not to yield.

The Christian man is sustained by the hope of the ageless life, "for which cause we faint not; but though our outward man perish, yet the inward man is renewed day by day." One of the finest things on old age that I have ever heard was a remark made to me by an honorable and aged Philadelphia physician who had retired to end his days at his ancestral home in Lancaster County, Pennsylvania. What he said to me was this: "So many ways to take in life. Now there is just one. So many teachers I have had in life. Now just one is necessary—the Holy Spirit."

Fear of Temptation and Sin

The fear of temptation is a worthy fear, for to fear to do wrong is a protection against sin. I once received a letter from a sailor in the Navy telling of a particular temptation to which he was subject and against which he was struggling, and how he feared that in spite of his prayers and better purpose, he might yield to the temptation. I told him that he must face this temptation with courage, and resist it at its first approach.

That was the way that Jesus dealt with the temptation of the Devil in the wilderness. He immediately answered the temptation with a verse from the Old Testament. The reason many go down before temptation's assault is that they delay to resist it at its first approach. To parley with the tempter, to turn the temptation over in one's mind, is to open the door to ruin.

I told the sailor to remember also that with the help of God and the determination of the mind, temptation can be conquered. As the apostle said, "There hath no temptation taken you but such as is common to man: but God is faithful, who will not suffer you to be tempted above that ye are able; but will with the temptation also make a way to escape, that ye may be able to bear it."

I reminded this sailor also of what Joseph said when he was tempted in a like manner, "How then can I do this great wickedness, and sin against God?" Prayer is the great defense against temptation. It not only unmasks the face of temptation, but gives us strength when we fight against an evil thing. When Satan entered the Garden of Eden to tempt man, the angel Ithuriel, according to Milton, discovered him in the form of a toad and touched him with the point of his spear. The moment he did that, Satan rose up in all his malice.

We must put our trust, too, when we fear temptation, in the promises of God. He has promised to deliver us. "Call upon me in the day of trouble: I will deliver thee." At the end of his brief, but mighty, epistle in which he speaks of the many great evils which assail the church and the Christian believer, and against which he warns the believer, Jude says: "Now unto him that is able to keep you from falling, and to present you faultless before the presence of his glory with exceeding joy, to the only wise God our Savior, be glory and majesty, dominion and power, both now and ever. Amen."

By the fear of sin, I mean the fear of past sin and the consequences of it, and fear of judgment to come upon sin. The first form in which fear assailed man was the fear of past sin. When the first man after his transgression heard the voice of God walking in the garden, he was afraid and hid himself among the trees of the garden. "Thus conscience does make cowards of us all." When sin has been committed, there is the fear of exposure. The wicked flee when no man pursueth.

There is also the fear of the future judgment. In view of what God has said about sin, we do well to fear those future judgments. We do well to say with the psalmist, "I am afraid of thy judgments."

God's beautiful and sublime remedy for sin and for the fear of sin, past and present, and the judgments upon sin, is forgiveness. "There is forgiveness with thee, that thou mayest be feared." What if God let us sin, but would not let us repent? What if he let us go from him and did not call us back to him?

A young woman, reaching out after reality in her Christian faith and troubled with the recollection of definite and specific sin, wrote me in great distress and asked, "Can Christ do anything for my sin?" Yes, Christ can do everything for sin. He can break the power of sin in your life. He can forgive sin by bearing the penalty of sin himself, and he can wash out the stain of sin.

These, then, are the fears which attack us in life, and these are the defenses against fear. The ideal society as described in the Bible is one where there is no fear. It is a society where everyone shall sit under his own vine and fig tree and "none shall make them afraid." It is the true condition of happiness.

When I read those great "no mores" in the book of Revelation, where the heavenly life is described, and where there is "no more sea," that is, the sea of unrest, and "no more tears," and "no more death," "no more curse," "no more night," "no more pain," I feel that I would like to add another great "no more"—"There shall be no more fear." When Christ was born at Bethlehem, that was what the angel said to the shepherds, "Fear not." Christ came to banish fear. Over the portals of heaven are written these words, greeting man as he enters the heavenly city, "Fear not!"

At the time of the Dunkirk disaster in 1940, when all Britain was shaken with the dread of the German invasion, someone wrote this inscription over the entrance to the Hind's Head Hotel near Dover: "Fear knocked. Faith answered, No one is here."

"God hath not given us the spirit of fear; but . . . of love, and of a sound mind." As one of the old hymns puts it so well:

> Henceforth the majesty of God revere.
> Fear him, and you have nothing else to fear.

The psalmist said, "What time I am afraid, I will trust in thee." That is good, very good. But still better is what Isaiah said, "I will trust, and not be afraid."

When Jesus was sleeping peacefully that night on the pillow in the stern of the ship, and the wind was howling and the waves were roaring, the frightened disciples awakened him and asked, "Carest thou not that we perish?" Jesus then arose and rebuked the wind and the waves, and there was a great calm. Then he turned to the disciples and said, "Why are ye so fearful? how is it that ye have no faith?" With Christ on the ship with them, the winds and the waves could not hurt them. Faith is the victory that overcometh the world. Faith is the victory that conquers fear.

NOTES

NOTES

NOTES

The Fixed Heart in the Day of Frightfulness

George Campbell Morgan (1863-1945) was the son of a British Baptist preacher, and he preached his first sermon when he was 13 years old. He had no formal training for the ministry, but his tireless devotion to the study of the Bible helped him to become one of the leading Bible teachers of his day. Rejected by the Methodists, he was ordained into the Congregational ministry. He was associated with Dwight L. Moody in the Northfield Bible conferences and as an itinerant Bible teacher. He is best known as the pastor of the Westminster Chapel, London (1904-17 and 1933-45). During his second term there, he had Dr. D. Martyn Lloyd-Jones as his associate. Morgan published more than 60 books and booklets, and his sermons are found in *The Westminster Pulpit* (London, Pickering and Inglis). This sermon is from Volume 10.

George Campbell Morgan

5

THE FIXED HEART IN THE DAY OF FRIGHTFULNESS

He shall not be afraid of evil tidings: His heart is fixed, trusting in the Lord (Psalm 112:7).

THE FIRST PART of the text describes a most desirable state of mind, that of being able to hear evil tidings without trembling and without panic. The second part of the text reveals the secret of such fearlessness. It is that of the fixed heart, and of the heart fixed because it has confidence in God.

This is supremely a day of evil tidings. Our newspapers are full of them. They contain nothing else. Their good news, the good news for which we look, and which comes to us ever and anon, is always laden with anguish. Battles won mean hearts broken. The tide of sorrow is rising higher and higher in the national life, and its dark waters are overflowing into every hamlet and every home. But they are especially emphatic, these newspapers of ours, about the tidings which are wholly evil. They tell us that the Government is incapable and weak, that politicians are corrupt, that generals are incapable, or, to summarize, that all the wise men are out of office. These are evil tidings, because for the most part they are untrue.

But there are other tidings coming to us day by day. The situation in one place is critical, the position in another is uncertain, the peril of the sea is not over. Well, these tidings are evil, because there is an element of truth, perchance, in the whole of them. These are the tidings that assault the soul, the mind, the heart, day by day.

Is it possible under such circumstances to be free from panic? Can broken hearts still be courageous? Can minds assaulted by panic-stricken rumor still be fearless? Can wills be dauntless in the presence of great perils? The answer of the text to these inquiries is that there is a man who is unafraid of evil tidings, and that the secret of that man's quietness is this: "his heart is fixed, trusting in the Lord." Let us, first, look at this man; and then let us consider the secret of his fearlessness in the midst of circumstances that make for fear.

The whole of the psalm from which the text is taken is in celebration of this man; and it is closely related to the preceding one. Both are acrostic psalms in the Hebrew Bible; each has twenty-two lines, and each line in every case commences with a letter of the Hebrew alphabet.

Their relationship is patent. Psalm 111 celebrates Jehovah. Psalm 112 celebrates the man who trusts in Jehovah. A most interesting exercise is to read them together, that is, to read verse one of Psalm 111, then verse one in 112, and so on throughout. Such a reading will reveal that all the things of excellence and glory and beauty celebrated in Jehovah are found also in the man who trusts in Him, and is obedient to Him.

Observe the closing of the first of these psalms and the opening of the second, for there we have an immediate indication of relationship. The psalm that celebrates the glory of Jehovah ends in these words:

> The fear of the Lord is the beginning of wisdom;
> A good understanding have all they that do thereafter;
> His praise endureth forever.

And the next psalm opens:

> Praise ye the Lord.
> Blessed is the man that feareth the Lord,
> That delighteth greatly in His commandments.

Psalm 112, then, is a character sketch; it is the revelation of a man. It is as beautiful as anything in literature. One wonders whether the writer knew some one man of whom he was thinking. Be that as it may, a man is in view, whether actual or ideal, and it is of this man that the words of our text are employed:

> He shall not be afraid of evil tidings;
> His heart is fixed, trusting in the Lord.

Now, we must see this man. Let me try to describe him as he is here described by the psalmist, but in other words.

The first thing I notice about him is the fact with which the singer opens:

He Is a God-fearing Man

Blessed is the man that feareth the Lord,
That delighteth greatly in His commandments.

So read the first verse of the psalm. My phrase is a much more modern one: he is a God-fearing man. He is a man whose first thought is Godward, a man whose whole life is lived under the mastery of the supreme and fundamental fact that he believes in God. This man may regularly, once or twice a week, or more often, say: "I believe in God the Father Almighty"; or he may hardly ever recite the creed in that particular form, but that is the truth about him. He is a God-fearing man.

The next thing I observe about him is this:

He Is a Home-making Man

His children shall be mighty upon earth:
The generation of the upright shall be blessed.
Wealth and riches are in his house,

(Remember these qualities are often found, in the high sense of the words, in the cottage as well as in the castle.)

And his righteousness endureth forever.

His seed mighty in the earth, his generation blessed among the sons of men—wealth and riches in his house are set in relationship to righteousness. He is the home-making man, the man who, first believing in God, has realized, in the deepest of life, though it may be that he does not often talk about it, that God's first circle of human society is the home and the family. He is a home-making man.

The next thing I observe is that—

He Is a Helping Man

Unto the upright there ariseth light in the darkness.

Let me say at once that this translation misses the

point of the declaration, which really is that this man ariseth unto the upright as light in the darkness. He is a center from which light flashes out on the way of other men. Notice what follows: "He is gracious, and full of compassion, and righteous." "He dealeth graciously and lendeth"; and yet again, presently,

> He hath dispersed, he hath given to the needy;
> His righteousness endureth forever.
> He is a man who is helping other men.

Finally, I observe one other thing about him:

He Is a Hated Man

> The wicked shall see it, and be grieved;
> He shall gnash with his teeth, and melt away.

This, then, is the man; he is a God-fearing man, a home-making man, a man who is always helping other people, a man who is hated by wicked men. Of that man the psalmist says:

> He shall not be afraid of evil tidings,
> His heart is fixed, trusting in the Lord.

Let us watch him in the day of evil tidings. What will he do? He gets the news of battle and of death! His heart is stricken, but he does not tremble. He reads his newspaper, and then puts it down, and goes on with his duty. If that man should be destroyed in an air raid, it will be at his post, and he will meet death cheerfully. "He shall not be afraid of evil tidings, his heart is fixed."

Whether this man was a man in the olden time on whom the psalmist looked, or whether he is the man you know, your father, perchance, he is a strong man, and all men know it. How is his strength to be accounted for?

And so we pass to consider the second part of the text, the revelation of the secret of this man's fearlessness:

His Heart Is Fixed

First, "His heart is fixed." Men who are strong are always men who are fixed somewhere, who have a conviction from which they cannot be separated by argument, which cannot be changed, whatever the circumstances in the midst of which they live. Sometimes these men are very narrow, but they are wonderfully strong; they are singularly obstinate, but they are splendidly dependable. Sometimes their convictions resolve themselves into two or three great fundamental truths, and they are never moved from them. Consequently, we always know where to find those men.

The fixed heart is the secret of courage. Courage is an affair of the heart; courage is the consciousness of the heart that is fixed. The positive is sometimes best illuminated by the negative. Therefore, let me say that men not so fixed are weak men, however strong they may be. I cannot better illustrate here than by a quotation from old Jacob. When Jacob was dying, he looked out on all his sons, and described them.

Note particularly his description of Reuben, and do not begin where people generally begin, "Unstable as water, thou shalt not excel." We must go further back. "Reuben, thou art my firstborn, my might, and the beginning of my strength; the excellency of dignity, and the excellency of power. Unstable as water, thou shalt not have the excellency." Was there ever a more graphic picture of the failure of a strong man than that? Reuben, thou art the excellency of dignity, thou art the excellency of power, thou art the beginning of my strength; thou shalt not have the excellency, thou shalt not enter into the inheritance of thine own possession! Why? Thou art *unstable* as water!

The man, who potentially was a great man, was weak and vacillating because his heart was not fixed, he had laid hold on nothing that was eternal and positive! Such a man drifts, is moved by every wind that sweeps over the surface of the sea, is unstable as water. That man is afraid in the day of evil tidings; that man leaves his post of duty when he expects an air raid; that man talks in the market place, and everywhere, about the failure of the Government and the failure of the politicians and the failure of the generals! Such a man is a menace to the State, and a hindrance to the purposes of God. His heart is not fixed; he has no central secret of power. He may be dynamic, he may be energetic, but he is not fixed. He is full of power, full of activity in certain directions, but he lacks that secret strength that enables his power to operate to purpose and to victory, and that keeps him strong in the shock of battle, in tempest and hurricane.

We leave him, and by the contrast we see more clearly this old-fashioned man, this God-fearing man, this home-making man, this man who is always willing to help someone else, this man who is hated by evil men, and so is highly complimented. This man is not afraid of evil tidings, because his heart is fixed.

The supreme value of this declaration, however, is that the psalmist has defined the fixity, "His heart is fixed, trusting in the Lord." This man finds his strength in the fact that at all times he maintains in his thinking the central and fundamental relationships of his life; *he trusts in the Lord.* Again, to use the negative method of illustration, his heart is not fixed, trusting in himself, but is fixed, trusting in the God Who explains what he is within himself, the God to Whom he himself is related.

In a certain way this man has no confidence in himself at all. In another way this man is perfectly confident of his ability to do the thing that God has appointed he should do; and he will do it, whatever storms may sweep, yea, though the mountains be removed and cast into the midst of the sea. He will not go on tour to watch them falling in the sea. He will stay where he is, and do his duty in the midst of the clash. He is trusting in the Lord, not in himself. And yet again, the fixity that characterizes the man described by the psalmist is not of confidence in circumstances. A man who is not confident in circumstances is careless about them.

If a man sees only the things that are happening, then, if they are not going according to his idea, he is perturbed, filled with fear—evil tidings render him hopeless. But if a man sees that there is a God controlling all circumstances, then, if circumstances are characterized by turmoil, so that nothing seems in place or in order, he is still unafraid, because he knows that circumstances are the arrangement of God. Therefore this man, trusting in God, knows that while he abides at his post, in the midst of the turmoil, the last word is not the word *turmoil*, but the word of the God Who is presiding over it. "His heart is fixed, trusting in the Lord."

And so one is driven to inquire: Who is this Lord in Whom this man trusts? Who is the God Whom this man fears, and in the fear of Whom he makes strong his own home, holds out helping hands to all who need his help, and because of these things is hated of wickedness? We go back again to Psalm 111, and there we find no doctrine of God, so far as a declaration of the mystery of His Being is concerned, but He is celebrated in the things He does, and by these things He is made known. The psalmist says of Him, "The works of the Lord are great," and "His work is honor and majesty."

Here are two words, the light and shadow of which we miss in our reading. Great are the things done! Majestic and honorable is the thing made! The psalmist says of Him that He "is gracious and full of compassion," that He is faithful to His covenants with His people; that He is true and just in all His deeds. Evil tidings come to the man who trusts in his God, tidings of death, tidings of disaster, tidings of difficulty; but the man knows by what he knows of God, not so much in character as in history, that God is overruling. The man knows that God is great in His doing, that He is majestic and stately in the things that He makes to be, that He is in Himself gracious and compassionate, that He is faithful to His covenants, that He is true and just in His deeds, and, therefore, the man is not afraid.

Come back again to the second of these psalms, and observe the effect of this knowledge on the character of the man. This fixity of heart results in fixity of character, and that fixity may be expressed in the two simplest phrases possible. This man is a man in whom there burns persistently a passion for righteousness and a pity for all need. "Holy and reverend is His name," sings the psalmist of the God in Whom the man trusts, and when he comes to write of the man who trusts in the Lord, the references

to the righteousness of the man run throughout. The God
in Whom this man believes is the God of unsullied and
undeviating holiness, and, therefore, the passion of this
man's life is a passion for truth and righteousness. But
the God in Whom this man believes is also a God full of
compassion and tender mercy, and, therefore, the man
who believes in Him becomes God's distributing center:
he scatters, distributes, and helps. His own heart fixed in
the God of holiness, he stands for righteousness in human
affairs. His own heart homed in the infinite compassion of
Deity, he stands for pity and grace and tenderness in the
sons of men. Consequently, he is not afraid of evil tidings.

Mark the reasonableness of his quietness, and observe
the expression of it. There comes to that man the tidings
of death. His own boy is gone! He is not callous. The
wound is full of pain, but there is no panic, there is no
trembling, there is no whining. He is not afraid, because
he knows that death is not the final news, that beyond
death, even in that tragic form, all the meaning of life is
discovered. He will fold his arms for a moment, perchance
ceasing his work while his bosom heaves, but he will say,
"He shall not return to me, but I shall go to him." His
heart is not afraid of evil tidings.

He also knows that the tidings of incompetence is not
the last word. God has always had to deal with human
incompetence, and he overrules it in order to arrive at His
own goal, to realize the destiny He purposes for humanity.
Where have we as a nation ever arrived as the result of
our own competence, tell me? We have arrived at wonderful
places of power, influence, and responsibility. If the Lord
had not been on our side, however, we should have failed!
If we will but read our history aright, we shall find it to
be a story of the overruling of incompetence by God; and
that it is this that has brought us to the position of power
and influence we have occupied in the world, and shall
still occupy if our feet are but turned back to the way of
His commandments, and our heart becomes fixed, trusting
in the Lord. The "fixed" man says, there may be much
incompetence, but the last word is God. Thus his heart is
not afraid of evil tidings.

And so, finally, to this man the tidings of danger is not

the only tidings. Like the ancient prophet, he has heard other tidings. Do you remember how Obadiah began that weird prophecy of the doom of Edom, the doom of the nation that trusted in its might and its frightfulness? Listen to this: "We have heard tidings from the Lord." Tidings from the Lord! These are the tidings which this man hears every morning. He reads something before he reads his newspaper—he has read his Bible. The man who is reading his newspaper and listening to the clamor of the voices speaking of failure and disaster and incapacity, and is not afraid, is the man who listens in the morning for another Voice, and goes to his work in the halls of legislature, in the mine, in the training camp drilling, in the home toiling, in the battle fighting, and as he goes he says, "We have heard tidings from the Lord."

What are the tidings from the Lord? Well, this is what God said concerning Edom:

> Behold, I have made thee small among the nations:
> thou art greatly despised. The pride of thine heart
> hath deceived thee, O thou that dwellest in the cleft
> of the rock, whose habitation is high; that saith in
> his heart, Who shall bring me down to the ground?
> Though thou mount on high as the eagle, and though
> thy nest be set among the stars, I will bring thee
> down from thence, saith the Lord.

The man who has heard those tidings from the Lord goes out and does his work, and is not afraid of evil tidings; his heart is fixed, trusting in the Lord.

Now, let us take up our newspapers again, and what do we see? We see a combination of words that I hardly know how to read! The Casualty List. By a wonderful spiritual instinct, hardly conscious, but coming up out of the subconsciousness of our national life, even our newspapers are putting something else; instead of Casualty List, we read Roll of Honor. They fall, our sons, our brothers, our lovers, our friends! We mourn, we grieve, we sorrow. We read these evil rumors, but we have heard tidings from the Lord, and, consequently, we are not afraid. We hear of grave situations, of peoples still confused, not knowing whether to pass to the right or to the left, to take this side or that side. We hear of diplomacies attempting to capture them for one side or the other. But, in spite of all, we are not afraid. And why not? We can best express it in the language of Julia Ward Howe:

> Mine eyes have seen the glory of the coming of the
> Lord. . . .
> He is sifting out the hearts of men before His
> judgment seat.

That, verily, is what He is doing. I am no prophet or the son of a prophet in the sense of predicting things to come; but I declare that when presently the war is over, and the conflict is done, we shall sit down quietly and see how these nations dropped into line, howsoever they may go, by virtue of what they were in their own heart and soul. God is compelling them to express themselves, and will do so to the end. If the only thing I see is what the diplomatists are doing, or not doing, then my heart is filled with fear; but when I see God sifting out the hearts of men before His judgment seat, then I continue with Julia Ward Howe, and I say:

> Oh, be swift, my soul, to answer Him!
> Be jubilant my feet!
> Our God is marching on.

What, then, shall we do in the day of frightfulness? We will do our duty, the thing that lies nearest, the thing we have to do tomorrow morning. We will do that, and do it well, and do it cheerfully. We will leave the rest to God, the sorrow, the suffering, and the issues. What this nation needs just now as much as, and perhaps more than, anything else is the multiplication of strong, quiet souls who are not afraid of evil tidings, who will go quietly to rest, no matter what may be coming, and will not add to the panic that demoralizes, but will do their work. The men and women who can do that on such a day are the men and women who have hearts *fixed*, trusting in Jehovah. May God make us such men and such women.

NOTES

NOTES

NOTES

Christ and the Fear of Death

George H. Morrison (1866-1928) assisted the great
Alexander Whyte in Edinburgh, pastored two churches,
and then became pastor in 1902 of the distinguished
Wellington Church on University Avenue in Glasgow. His
preaching drew great crowds; in fact, people had to line
up an hour before the services to be sure to get seats in
the large auditorium. Morrison was a master of
imagination in preaching, yet his messages are solidly
biblical. From his many published volumes of sermons, I
have chosen this message, found in *The Afterglow of God*,
published in 1912 by Hodder and Stoughton, London.

George H. Morrison

6

CHRIST AND THE FEAR OF DEATH

And deliver them who through fear of death were all their lifetime subject to bondage (Hebrews 2:15).

THERE ARE TWO feelings which the thought of death has ever kindled in the human breast, and the first of them is curiosity. Always in the presence of that veil, through which sooner or later we all pass, men have been moved to ask, with bated breath, What is it which that veil conceals? It is as if the most diaphanous of curtains were hung between our eye and the great secret, making men the more wistful to interpret it. It has been said by a well-known Scottish essayist that this would account for the crowd at executions. You know how the people used to flock in thousands when a criminal was to die upon the gallows. And Alexander Smith throws out this thought that it was not just savagery which brought them there. It was the unappeasable curiosity which death forever stirs in human hearts.

But if the thought of death moves our curiosity, there is another feeling which is ever linked with it. Death is not alone the source of wonder. Death has ever been the source of fear. How universal that feeling is we see from this, that we share it with all animate creation. Wherever there is life in any form there is an instinct which recoils from death. When the butterfly evades the chasing schoolboy—when the stag turns at bay against the dogs—we have the rudiments of that which in a loftier sphere may grow to be a bondage and a tyranny. The fear of death is not a religious thing, although religion has infinitely deepened it. It is as old as existence; as wide as the whole world; as lofty and deep as the whole social fabric. It touches the native in the heart of Africa, as every reader of Dr. Livingstone knows, and it hides under the mantle of the prince as well as under the jacket of the prodigal. How keenly it was felt in the old world, every reader of pagan literature has seen. The aim and object of the old philosophy was largely to crush it out of human life. In the great and gloomy poem of Lucretius, in many a page of Cicero, above all in the treatises of Plutarch and of Seneca, we learn what a mighty thing the fear of death was with the men and women of the Roman Empire.

The Fact of Death Ignored

Of course I do not mean that the fear of death is always active and present and insistent. To say that would be exaggeration, and would be untrue to the plain facts of life. When a man is in the enjoyment of good health, he very rarely thinks of death at all. When the world goes well with him and he is happy, he has the trick of forgetting he is mortal. He digs his graves within the garden walls, and covers them with a wealth of summer flowers, so that the eye scarce notices the mound when the birds are singing in the trees. We know, too, how a passion or enthusiasm will master the fear of death within the heart.

A soldier in the last rush will never think of it, though comrades are dropping on every side of him. And a timid mother, for her little child's sake, or a woman for the sake of one she loves, will face the deadliest peril without trembling. For multitudes the fear of death is dormant, else life would be unbearable and wretched. But though it is dormant it is always there, ready to be revived in the last day. In times of shipwreck—in hours of sudden panic—when we are ill and told we may not live, then shudderingly, as from uncharted deeps, there steals on men this universal terror. Remember there is nothing cowardly in that. A man may be afraid and be a hero. There are times when to feel no terror is not courage. It is but the hall-mark of insensibility.

It is not what a man feels that makes the difference. It is how he handles and orders what he feels. It is the spirit in which he holds himself, in the hour when the heart is overwhelmed.

Nor can we be altogether blind to the purposes which

God meant this fear to serve. Like everything universal in the heart, it has its office in the plans of heaven. You remember the cry wrung from the heart of Keats in his so exquisite music to the nightingale. "Full many a time," he sings, "I have been half in love with easeful death." And it may be that there are some here tonight who have been at times so weary of it all, that they too have been in love with easeful death. It may have been utter tiredness that caused it. It may have been something deeper than all weariness. Who knows but that even here before me there be not someone who has dreamed of suicide?

Brethren, it is from all such thoughts, and from all the passion to have done with life, that we are rescued and redeemed and guarded by the terror which God has hung around the grave. Work may be hard, but death is harder still. Duty may be stern, but death is sterner. Dark and gloomy may be the unknown morrow, but it is not so dark and gloomy as the grave. Who might not break the hedge and make for liberty were the hedge easy to be pushed aside? But God has hedged us about with many a thorn—and we turn to our little pasturage again.

When Adam and Eve had been expelled from Eden, they must have longed intensely to return. It was so beautiful, and the world so desolate; it was so fertile, and the world so hard. But ever, when they clasped repentant hands, and stole in the twilight to the gate of Paradise, there rose the awful form with flaming sword. Sleepless and vigilant he stood at watch. His was a dreadful and terrific presence. No human heart could face that living fire which stood in guardianship of what was lost. And that was why God had placed his angel there, that they might be driven back to the harsh furrow, and till the soil, and rise into nobility, while the sweat was dropping from the brow. So are we driven back to life again by the terror which stands sentinel to death. So are we driven to our daily cross, however insupportable it seems. And bearing it, at first because we must, it comes to blossom with the passing days, till we discover that on this side the grave there is more of paradise than we had dreamed.

Christ then does *not* deliver us from the deep instinct

of self-preservation. That is implanted in the heart by God. It is given for the safeguarding of his gift. It is only when that fear becomes a bondage, and when that instinct grows into a tyranny, that Christ steps in, and breaks the chains that bind us, and sets our trembling feet in a large room. The question is, then, how did he do that? How has Christ liberated us from this bondage? I shall answer that by trying to distinguish three elements which are inherent in that fear.

Death and Dying

In the first place, our fear of death is in a measure but a fear of dying. It is not the fact of death which terrified; it is all that we associate with the fact. We may have seen some death-bed which was a scene of agony; it is memory which we shall never lose. We may have read, in a novel or in a play, a story of torment in the closing hours. And it is not what death leads to or removes, but rather that dark accompanying prospect, which lies hidden within a thousand hearts as an element of the terror of the grave. I think I need hardly stop to prove to you that this is an unreasonable fear. If there are death-beds which are terrible, are there not others which are quiet as sleep? But blessed be God, Christ does not only comfort us when we are terrified with *just* alarms: he comforts us when we are foolish children. Girt with mortality, he says to us, "Take no anxious thought about the morrow." Dreading the pain that one day may arrive, he says, "Sufficient unto the day is its own evil." He never prayed, "Give us a sight of death, and help us to contemplate it every hour we live." He prayed, "Give us this day our daily bread." Christ will not have us stop the song today, because of the possible suffering tomorrow. If we have grace to live by when we need it, we shall have grace to die by when we need it. And so he sets his face against that element, and says to us, "Let not your heart be troubled." "My grace shall be sufficient for thee, and my strength made perfect in thy weakness."

Is Death the End?

Secondly, much of our fear of death springs from the

thought that death is the end of everything. It is always pitiful to say farewell, and there is no farewell like that of death. You remember how Charles Lamb uttered that feeling, with the wistful tenderness which makes us love him. He did not want to leave this kindly world, nor his dear haunts, nor the familiar faces. And deep within us, though we may not acknowledge it, there is that factor in the fear of death—the passionate clinging of the human heart to the only life which it has known. We have grown familiar with it in the years. It has come to look on us with friendly eyes. It has been a glad thing to have our work to do, and human love and friendship have been sweet. And then comes death, and takes all that away from us, and says it never shall be ours again, and we brood on it, and are lonely and afraid.

Thanks be to God, *that* factor in the fear has been destroyed by Jesus Christ. For he has died, and he is risen again, and he is the first-fruits of them that sleep. And if the grave for him was not an end, but only an incident in life eternal, then we may rest assured that in his love there is no such sadness as the broken melody. All we have striven to be we shall attain. All we have striven to do we shall achieve. All we have loved shall meet us once again with eyes that are transfigured in the dawn. Every purpose that was baffled here, and every love that never was fulfilled, all that, and all our labor glorified, shall still be ours when shadows flee away.

This life is but the prelude to the piece. This life is the introduction to the book. It is not *finis* we should write at death. It is not *finis*, it is *initium*. And that is how Jesus Christ has met this element, and mastered it in his victorious way, and made it possible for breaking hearts to bear the voiceless sorrow of farewell.

Of Death and Judgment

Thirdly, much of the fear of death springs from the certainty of coming judgment. Say what you will, you know as well as I do that there is a day of judgment still to come. Conscience tells it, if conscience be not dead. The very thought of a just God demands it. Unless there be a judgment still to come, life is the most tragical of mockeries. And every voice of antiquity proclaims it, and every savage tribe within the forest; and with a certainty that never wavered it was proclaimed by the Lord Jesus Christ. Well may you and I fear death, if "after death, the judgment." Seen to our depths, with every secret known, we are all to stand before Almighty God. Kings will be there, and peasants will be there, and you and I who are not kings nor peasants. And the rich and the poor will meet together there, for the Lord is the maker of them all. It is that thought which makes death so terrible. It is that which deepens the horror of the tomb.

Dwell on that coming day beyond the grave, and what prospect of affright it is! And it is then that Jesus Christ appears, and drives these terrors to the winds of heaven, and says to the vilest sinner here tonight, "Son of man, stand upon thy feet." He that believeth *hath* everlasting life. He gives us our acquittal here and now. He tells us that for every man who trusts him there is now therefore no condemnation. And he tells us that because he died for us, and because he bore our sins up to the tree, and because he loves us with a love so mighty that neither life nor death can tear us from it. That is the faith to live by and to die by: "I will both lay me down in peace and sleep." That is the faith which makes us more than conquerors over the ugliest record of our past. O death, where is thy sting? O grave, where is thy victory? Thanks be to God, who giveth us the victory through our Lord Jesus Christ.

NOTES

NOTES

NOTES

Fear Not

Charles Haddon Spurgeon (1834-1892) is undoubtedly the most famous minister of modern times. Converted in 1850, he united with the Baptists and soon began to preach in various places. He became pastor of the Baptist church in Waterbeach in 1851, and three years later he was called to the decaying Park Street Church, London. Within a short time, the work began to prosper, a new church was built and dedicated in 1861, and Spurgeon became London's most popular preacher. In 1855, he began to publish his sermons weekly; and today they make up the fifty-seven volumes of *The Metropolitan Tabernacle Pulpit*. He founded a pastor's college and several orphanages. This sermon is taken from *The Metropolitan Tabernacle Pulpit*, volume 26.

Charles Haddon Spurgeon

7

FEAR NOT

Fear not (Revelation 1:17).

"FEAR NOT" IS A PLANT which grows very plentifully in God's garden. If you look through the lily beds of Scripture you will continually find by the side of other flowers the sweet "Fear nots" peering out from among doctrines and precepts, even as violets look up from their hiding places of green leaves. "Fear nots" bloomed in the old time, at the feet of Abraham, when he returned from the fighting with the kings. Melchizedek blessed him, and the Lord comforted him. The patriarch might have been half afraid that he would always lead a troubled life, now that he had once drawn the sword; but the Lord came to him in vision, and said, "Fear not, Abram. I am thy shield, and thy exceeding great reward." If he had to undergo a soldier's toils, he should have a soldier's shield and a soldier's pay, and both should be exceeding great, for he should find them both in God. After you have been fighting battles for Christ you may feel weary and worried, and then your great Melchizedek will refresh you with bread and wine, and whisper in your ear "Fear not."

A "Fear not" was spoken to Isaac when he had dug wells, and the Philistines strove for them, and he, like the meek soul that he was, gave them up one by one to avoid a conflict. At last he settled down at Beersheba, and there the Lord appeared unto him, and said, "Fear not, for I am with thee, and will bless thee." He was a feeble man, and therefore the Lord dealt tenderly with him. If any of you are meek and quiet spirits, and rather apt to tremble exceedingly, may the Lord often give you a blessed "Fear not" to wear in your bosoms, that its fragrance may comfort your hearts. Then there was Jacob. You know how troubled his life was, but when he heard that his beloved son whom he thought was dead was alive in Egypt, and was clothed with glory, and that he had sent for him to go down to see him, he was afraid to go till the Lord said to him, "Fear not to go down into Egypt," and gave him this encouraging promise, "I will go down with thee into Egypt."

If any of you are making a great change in life and moving, perhaps, to the very ends of the earth, "fear not to go down into Egypt." Should God command you to go to the utmost verge of the green earth, to rivers unknown to song, yet if he bids you go, fear not to go down into Egypt, for certainly he will be with you.

The Israelites at the Red Sea were afraid of Pharaoh, and then the Lord said to them, "Fear not, stand still and see the salvation of God." If you are brought to a pass tonight, and know not what to do, take the advice of Holy Scripture, and "Fear not"; but "stand still and see the salvation of God." As we observe the Scriptures we perceive that "Fear nots" are scattered throughout the Bible as the stars are sprinkled over the whole of the sky, but when we come to Isaiah we find constellations of them. When I was a boy I learned Dr. Watts's catechism, and I am glad I did. One of its questions runs thus, "Who was Isaiah?" And the answer is, "He was the prophet who spake more of Jesus Christ than all the rest." Very well, and for that very reason—that he spoke more of Jesus Christ than all the rest—he is richest in comfort to the people of God, and continually he is saying, "Fear not."

Here are a few of his antidotes for the fever of fear: "Say to them that are of a fearful heart, Be strong, fear not." "Fear thou not, for I am with thee; be not dismayed, for I am thy God." "Fear not, I will help thee." "Fear not, thou worm Jacob." "Fear not, I have redeemed thee." "Fear not, for thou shalt not be ashamed; neither be thou confounded, for thou shalt not be put to shame"; and so on, I was going to say, "world without end." So abundant are these "Fear nots" that they grow like the king-cups and the daisies, and other sweet flowers of the meadows, among which the little children in the spring-time delight themselves. As to gathering them all, no one would attempt the task. The bank that is fullest of these beautiful flowers is that which Isaiah has cast up; go there and pluck them for yourselves.

Now I gather from the plentifulness of "Fear nots," even in the Old Testament, that the Lord does not wish his people to be afraid, that he is glad to see his people full of courage, and especially that he does not love them to be *afraid of him.* He would have his children treat him with confidence. Slavish fear may be thought to be congenial to the Old Testament, and yet it is not so, for there the Lord cries to his chosen, "Fear not."

When we come into the New Testament, there we see God coming more familiarly to men than ever before; not descending upon Paran with ten thousand flaming chariots, setting the mountain on a blaze, but coming down to Bethlehem in an infant's form, with angels chanting the joyful lay, "Glory to God in the highest, and on earth peace, goodwill toward men." The genius of the New Testament is drawing near to God: ceasing to tremble and beginning to trust, ceasing to be the slave and learning to be the child. Though in the precise form of it the words of my text were not very often spoken by the Lord Jesus Christ, yet his whole life was one long proclamation of "Fear not."

I think I shall give you tonight most of the instances in which our Lord himself expressly said "Fear not," and as each one I shall give you will either come from the lip of Christ, or else from Christ's own angel, sent to comfort one of his servants, I pray that it may come fresh from God to every tried and troubled believer, and that all of us together may receive for our different fears this one same solace from the mouth of the Eternal, "Thus saith the Lord unto thee, fear not."

1. Our first text you will kindly look for if you have your Bibles with you. I hope you all have them, for I love to hear the rustling of Bible-leaves as we do in Scotland, but not often in England. Turn to Revelation 1:17, and there you will read that John beheld the Savior in his glorious array, and he says,

"When I saw him, I fell at his feet as dead. And he laid his right hand upon me, saying unto me, Fear not; I am the first and the last."

Fear Not His Majesty

Our first "Fear not" meets the dread occasioned by the majesty of our Savior's person. You who know him hold him in deepest reverence, even as John did when at the sight of his divine Lord he fell at his feet as dead. Did you ever think of Jesus as divine, and try to form some idea of his grandeur, his triumph, and his exaltation above the thrones and principalities of heaven? As your soul has extolled him, and your mind has been expanded with high thoughts of the all-glorious Son of God, has it not occurred to you to say within yourself, "How dare I think that he is my Beloved, and that I am his? Could such majesty meet such misery? Could such glory bring itself into union with such insignificance as mine?" I know you must have experienced that feeling; and yet you must not yield to it, for our Lord Jesus, although he loves to see your holy awe, would not have that reverence freeze into a chill reserve or a slavish trembling. No, though he be divine, he invites you to approach him without dread. Great as he is, you may dare to be free with him.

"Let us be simple with him then—
Not backward, stiff, or cold,
As though our Bethlehem could be
What Sinai was of old."

Let your Lord be glorious to you, but still let him be near you. Exalt him on his throne, but remember that you sit there with him. However glorious he may be, he has desired that you may behold his glory, and be with him where he is. To you hath he given to overcome, and to sit upon his throne even as he has overcome, and has sat down with the Father upon his throne.

If you have studied the matchless purity of his character with adoring admiration, you must have been amazed at the absolute perfection of his manhood, and the glory of his moral and spiritual character. At such times, if you have had a true sense of your own position, you have been ready to sink into the dust, and you have exclaimed, "Shall *he* wash my feet? Shall *he* give himself for me? Can it be that he could have loved one so stained and polluted, so mean and so beggarly, so altogether unworthy even to live, much less to be loved by such an altogether lovely one?" But I pray you always to remember, when you think of his perfection, that he has perfection of mercy as well as of holiness, and perfection of love to sinners as well as perfection of hatred of sin; and that, guilty as you are, you must never doubt his affection, for he has pledged you in his heart's blood, and proved his love by his death. Albeit that you are conscious of being less than nothing and vanity, and know that Jesus is absolute perfection, yet regard him not with timorous dread, but draw near to him as confidently as a child to its parent, or a wife to her husband. It is one of Satan's temptations to make us afraid of Christ. Let us not be ignorant of his devices.

Why should you be afraid of Jesus when he tells you not to be? Why dread the Lamb of God? *He* says, "Fear not." It is not the preacher who cries "Fear not," but it is Jesus himself who whispers to his poor servant, fallen as dead at his feet, "Fear not: fear not." It will be disobedience, then, to be afraid. When those lips, which are as lilies, dropping sweet-smelling myrrh, say to me, "Child of mine, fear not," how can I be afraid? Your safety lies, remember, dear friend, in trusting Jesus, and not in being afraid of him. There was never a soul yet saved by being afraid of Christ: there was never a prodigal that found forgiveness yet by being afraid of his Father. This kind of fear wants casting out, for it hath torment.

Jesus, our Lord, is great and good, but then he has chosen to become the Savior of sinners, and we need not fear to approach him, for "this man receiveth sinners." A host who entertains at his table the poorest of the poor and the lowest of the low, and bids them welcome, is not one to be feared. Remember that if you are honestly afraid of Jesus, you should be afraid of grieving him by being afraid of him. When the physician sees the patient shrinking from his knife he does not wonder, but when Jesus sees you shrinking from that hand which does not wound, but cures by its own wound, he looks with eyes of sorrow upon such fear. Why shrink from him? The little children ran into his arms. Why shrink from him? Nothing cuts him to the quick more than the unkind, ungenerous thought that he is unwilling to receive the guilty. If he meant to keep you at a distance he would have stopped in heaven; his coming here cannot mean anything else than love to the perishing: therefore do not grieve him by being afraid of him. Remember that his truthfulness forbids the rejection of any that ever come to him, since he has pledged his word that he will in no wise cast them out. You need not therefore be afraid that *you* especially may not come.

I had a letter but this week, in which one poor soul says, "I believe that I am the worst person that ever lived: though not in outward appearance, yet in heart. I believe that all other sorts of people feel more than I do, or have some one point in which they are better than I am, but I am the worst of all, and I fear that Jesus will never look on me." Downcast soul, there is no true ground for such a suspicion. If you had a devil in you, you might still come to Christ; and if there were a legion of devils in you—and I do not quite know how many made up a legion; but if there were so many that you could not count them—yet you might come with all the devils in hell in you and he still would not frown upon you, but he would cast the devils out of you. Oh, be not afraid to come to him whose wounds invite you. The blessed Savior who receiveth sinners loves not that you should stay away through fear.

I know what some of you are doing: you are trying to get to heaven by a roundabout road. The late Emperor of Russia, when the railway was to be made between Moscow and St. Petersburg, employed a great number of engineers in making plans. He looked over many of their maps, and at last, like the practical man that he was, he said, "Here, bring me a ruler." They brought him a ruler: he took a pencil, and drawing a straight line he said, "That is the way to engineer it: we want no other plan than one straight line."

There are a great many ways of engineering souls to heaven; but the only one that is worth considering is this:—Draw a straight line to Christ at once. Did I hear one awakened soul say, "I should like to talk to Mr. Cuff"? By all means talk to him, but do not stop *at* that, nor stop *for* that. Go to Christ first. "Oh, but I should like to talk with a good woman—a dear Christian lady." I recommend you to go to Jesus Christ at once, and see the lady afterwards. It is all very well to have an inquiry-room, and I have not a word to say against it, but the best inquiry-room in the world is your own bedroom. Go and inquire of Christ straight away.

We may make our Christian workers and leaders into little priests if we do not mind what we are at. There must be nobody between a soul and Christ. Blind souls will never get their eyes opened by all the kind hands of all the good people in Shoreditch, or in all London. Christ's hands can give sight, and only his; and you may get to Christ tonight. "Which way?" say you. By no movement of your body, but by a motion of your mind. Turn your thoughts towards him, your desires towards him, your trust towards him. Look to him and live. May the Holy Ghost lead you to trust him now, and he will save you.

Thus have I tried very briefly to set forth the fear which arises from the majesty of the divine person of Christ, for which he prescribes this cure: "Fear not, I am the first and the last: I am he that liveth and was dead; and behold I am alive forevermore." Do not be afraid of Jesus because of his glory, nor stand back because of your unfitness. You *do* want a Mediator between your soul and God; but you do *not* want a mediator between your souls and Christ. You may come to him straight away just as you are.

> Come needy, and guilty, come loathsome and bare;
> You can't come too filthy, come just as you are.

Draw a straight line,—remember that, a straight line from your lost condition to Christ, and let your resolve be: I, being lost, trust Jesus to save me, and I am saved.

Fear Not the Problem

The second "Fear not" is equally precious. Turn to Luke 8:50, the chapter we were reading just now, and there you will find that Jairus had a little daughter, who was dead, and they said—

"Trouble not the Master. But when Jesus heard it, he answered him, saying, Fear not: believe only, and she shall be made whole."

This meets the fear arising out of the desperateness of the case in hand. The little girl was actually dead; and yet Jesus said, "Fear not." Here is comfort *as to others.* Dear friend, if you have been praying for a long time about anyone who is near and dear to you, and you have been longing for that person's salvation, and your prayer has not been answered, and that person has even gone from bad to worse, I want you not to give up praying. "Oh, but," you say, "I am getting very downcast, for they are plunging into deeper sin." Well, there is cause for fear, but not while Jesus lives, for he can reach a soul so long as it remains this side the gates of death. Jesus can still save a man while he is yet out of hell. Continue to pray, and fear not.

No case is absolutely hopeless while Jesus lives. Love will still prevail. We meet sometimes with amazing instances where prayer is heard at last. I have read of a woman who prayed long for her husband. She used to attend a certain meeting-house in the north of England, but her husband never went with her. He was a drinking, swearing man, and she had much anguish of heart about him. She never ceased to pray, and yet she never saw any result. She went to the meeting-house quite alone, with this exception, that a dog always went with her, and this faithful animal would curl himself up under the seat, and lie quiet during the service. When she was dead, her husband was still unsaved, but doggie went to the meeting-house. His master wondered whatever the faithful animal did at the service. Curiosity made him follow the good creature. The dog led him down the aisle to his dear old mistress's seat. The man sat on that seat, and the dog curled himself up as usual. God guided the minister that day; the word came with power, and that man wept till he found the Savior.

Never give up on your husbands, good women, for the Lord may even use a dog to bring them to Christ when you are dead and gone. Never give up praying, hoping, and expecting. Fear not; believe only, and you shall have your heart's desire. Pray for them as long as there is breath in your body and theirs. It is of no use praying for them when they are dead, but as long as they are here never cease to plead with God on their account. Persons have been converted to God under very extraordinary circumstances.

Two base fellows thought to rob the house of a godly man, the vicar of the parish, who was accustomed on Sunday evening to gather his poor people together in his parlor and preach the gospel to them. This was a little extra work after the day's services. The thieves thought that if they could get into the house with the people during the evening, and hide themselves away, they could rob the house easily during the night; and so they got into the next room to that in which the Word was preached. But they never robbed that house, for through the godly vicar's address the Lord Jesus Christ stole away their hearts, and they came forth to confess their sin, and to become followers of the Savior. You do not know how far the arrows of the conquering Savior may fly. Never despair. Jesus Christ comforts you in reference to the souls of those for whom you are anxious, by saying "Fear not; believe only, and they shall be made whole." Labor for them, pray for them, and believe that Jesus Christ can save them.

Let the same truth be fully believed *as to yourselves.* O my dear hearer, you may think you are too far gone for salvation, but you are not. You may imagine that your case is altogether a lot out of the catalog; but you are just the sort of person that Jesus Christ saves. If he never saved odd people he would never have saved me, for many men judge me to be a singular being. If you are another oddity, come along with me, and let us trust in him.

If you are the one man that is a little over the line of mercy, you are the very man that Jesus Christ chooses to bless, for he loves to save extraordinary sinners. He is a very extraordinary Savior; there never was another like him, and when he meets a sinner that is extraordinary, and never another like him, he often takes him, and makes him one of his captains, as he did Saul of Tarsus, who became Paul the apostle. I do pray you "fear not" on account of the greatness of your sin. Be humbled on account of it, but do not despair about it.

Are you old in iniquity? Are you deeply ingrained in transgression by long practice in it? Still doubt not the Redeemer's power. If your salvation rested on yourself you might despair, but the Lord has laid help on one that is mighty, even on his only-begotten Son, and he is able to save to the uttermost them that come to God by him. O poor condemned sinner, look up and hope. O thou who hast heard the clang of the iron gate, thou who art shut up in despair, have hope, have brave hope, for Jesus saith to thee, "Fear not, believe only, and thou shalt be made whole." God grant that this gracious "Fear not" may be a comfort to some seeker here.

Fear Not His Goodness

Our third "Fear not" is taken from Luke 5:7, and perhaps what I am about to say will suit Mr. Cuff and other successful ministers:

"They came, and filled both the ships, so that they began to sink. When Simon Peter saw it, he fell down at Jesus' knees, saying, Depart from me; for I am a sinful man, O Lord. For he was astonished, and all that were with him, at the draught of the fishes which they had taken: And so was also James, and John, the sons of Zebedee, which were partners with Simon. And Jesus said unto Simon, Fear not; from henceforth thou shalt catch men."

This meets the fear which arises out of the greatness of his goodness. If the Lord has made any one of you successful in his service, if you are made of the same stuff as I am, your success lays you low before his throne. Time was when everybody was abusing me, and then I rejoiced and gloried in God: I had happy days when my name was cast out as evil. But when the Lord in his great mercy gave me souls for my hire, and began to build up the church at the Tabernacle, I became subject thereupon to such sinking of spirits that I can scarcely tell you how crushed I have been under the weight of divine mercy. I should not wonder if my dear brother Cuff has gone home, after seeing a crowd at the Town Hall, and after seeing this great house full, and has said, "Lord, why hast thou been pleased to use *me* and to favor *me?*" If any of you are blessed in your work, as I trust you may be, you may also be made to feel the mysterious depression which takes the place of self-exaltation in those who know that every good gift comes from God alone.

Fear because of the Lord's great goodness also comes in another shape: a person says, "I believe that I am saved for I have looked to Christ, and I am lightened. And yet can it be?" The thought suggests itself, "It is too good to be true." Now, look you, sirs, if it were not supremely good it would not be true. It is because it is so excessively good that it is true. As one said of God's mercy when his friend was astonished at it, "I am astonished too; but still it is just like him." It is just the way of God, you know, to bless a poor sinner beyond all that he can ask or think. It is the way with God to astonish us with his grace. When the Lord sends his mercy it never rains, but it pours. He deluges the desert. He not only gives enough to moisten, but enough to drench the furrows. He makes the wilderness a standing pool of water, and the thirsty land springs of water. Do not, therefore, doubt the genuineness of his mercy because of its greatness.

But some timorous professors say, "This is a great work which God is doing here, but it is too great to last." Yes, that too I have heard, and the gathering of many to hear the gospel has been sneered at as "a nine days' wonder." Alas! our unbelief has said, "It cannot last"; and yet it has lasted. The path of faith to my mind is very like that of a man walking on a tight-rope high up in the air, and you always seem half afraid that he will fall; yet if the Lord placed us on a spider's web as high as the Alps he would not let us slip.

The walk of faith is like going up an invisible staircase. When you have climbed and climbed, you sometimes cannot see one single step before you. Each step seems to be upon the air, and yet when you put your foot down it is solid granite firmer than the earth itself.

There are times when Satan whispers, "God will leave you. God will forsake you. He has done all this for you, and yet he will leave you." Ah, but he never will, for his faithfulness never fails. We must not be like the countryman who, when he had to cross the river, said that he would wait till the stream was dry, for it could not run so fast as that long, but must all run away. We have feared that we should live till the river of God's mercy had run dry; but it never has, and it never will.

Some professors say when a great number of sinners are converted, "Oh, well, you see there are so many, they cannot be all genuine." That is why I think the work to be real. When I see a little peddling work of one every now and then, I am far more inclined to say, "Well, I do not know. It may be of God, but it is not a very great affair, and he generally does great things when his Spirit is poured out." But when I see him calling three thousand in one day, I say, "This is the finger of God. I am sure of it."

I would be the last to despise the day of small things, but I must also speak up for the day of great things. I have noticed that those who are added to the church at times of revival are people who hold on quite as well as others, and I think better than others. That is my experience; because at other times we are apt to say, "There are so few coming forward; we must not be quite so strict in examining them"; but when there is a great number we feel that we can afford to be particular, and we are naturally more strict. I do not justify this, but I am sure that the tendency exists. I believe in a great work; and when I see our Lord filling the net, I think I hear him saying to me, "Do not be afraid because the fish make the boat sink down to the water's edge. Fear not, you shall get many more than these. Let down your net again."

Let us not doubt because it seems too wonderful that God should bless us to a great extent. It is wonderful, but let us have no doubt about it. Can the Lord use such poor worms as we are? He does use us. Do not ask how he can do it if he does do it. He is a God of sovereignty, and he uses whom he wills, and if he blesses you, give him the glory of it: but do not let the greatness of his grace cause you to mistrust. You have seen a painter with his palette on his finger, and he has ugly little daubs of paint upon the palette. What can he do with those spots? Go in and see his picture. What splendid painting! What lights! What shades! Where are those daubs of paint? They have been used up upon the picture. What! Did he make that picture out of those ugly spots of paint? Yes, that picture was made out of those little daubs of color!

That is the way with painters. In even a wiser way does Jesus act towards us. He takes us, poor smudges of paint, and he makes the blessed pictures of his grace out of us; for it is neither the brush he uses, nor the paint he uses, but it is the skill of his own hand which does it all, and unto his name be the praise.

Now, poor worker, do not be afraid. The great Artist will take you in hand, and make something of you. I forget how much can be made out of a pennyworth of iron, but I do know that there are methods by which a pennyworth of iron can be so molded, and wrought, and fashioned, that it can become worth a hundred times what it was before it came under the manufacturer's hand. What the Lord can make of such poor creatures as we are, who shall tell? He says, "Fear not"; and I pray you do not fear.

Fear and Persecution

But now I turn to a fourth "Fear not," which we find in the Matthew 10:28. I will not turn to it, but I will just tell you of it because there are many of you here who need its comfort.

"Fear not them which kill the body, but are not able to kill the soul: bur rather fear him which is able to destroy both soul and body in hell."

This is meant to remove the fear arising out of sharp persecution. In a region like this, when a working man is converted to Jesus Christ, his friends and his neighbors soon find it out, and I am sorry to say that working-men, as a rule, do not treat Christian men fairly. It is a free country, every man may swear at his fellow-workman for worshiping God. It is a fearful piece of meanness that men should molest their fellows for being godly. If you have a right to swear, I have a right to sing psalms; and if you have a right to break the Sabbath, I have a right to keep it, and I have a right to go in and out of the workshop without being called bad names because I live in the fear of God. But the right is not always recognized. Some have to run the gauntlet from morning to night because they serve the Lord. Now, my dear brothers and sisters in Christ, do not be afraid, though you are nothing but poor sheep, and you are sent out into the midst of wolves. Does it not seem as if our Lord could hardly have known what he was at when he said, "Behold, I send you forth as sheep among wolves"? Yet he made no mistake. Just think for a minute:—how many wolves are there in the world now? They have been eating up the sheep ever since they had a chance; but are there more wolves or more sheep alive at this day? Why, the wolves get fewer and fewer every day, till when a wolf comes down into the inhabited lands in France we have it reported in the paper, and we have not one animal of the kind in this country wild, though they used to abound here. The fact is, the sheep have driven out the wolves. It looked as if they would eat the sheep up, but the sheep have exterminated them. So it will be in the end with defenseless believers and raging persecutors; patient weakness will overcome passionate strength.

Only be patient. You have an anvil in the shop: and you know how hard the hammer comes down on it. What does the anvil do? Why, it bears it. You never saw the anvil get up and fight the hammer. Never. It stands still and takes the blows. Down comes the hammer. But now listen. How many hammers have been worn out to one anvil? Where it has stood for years, the old block of iron remains, ready to bear more strokes. The hammers will break, but not the anvil.

Be you an anvil, brother. Be you the sheep, brother, still; for heavenly submission shall win the victory, and patient non-resistance shall come off more than a conqueror.

Do not fear, I pray you, so as to conceal your testimony. Tell out for Jesus Christ what he has done for you, and the more they blaspheme and persecute you, be you the more determined by God's grace that they shall not be able to find fault in your character, and that they shall know that you are a Christian man. Climb up the mast and nail the colors to it. Drive another nail tonight. Fix the colors to the mast-head. Say, "No, never by God's grace will I be ashamed of being a Christian. I might be ashamed if I were a drunkard. I might be ashamed if I were a swearer; but I never will be ashamed that I am a follower of the crucified Son of God."

O poor men and women, who have for the most part to bear the brunt of the world's assaults, God grant that you may not fear. Do not fall into doubt about your religion either. Do not be so afraid as to fall into questioning and unbelief. True religion never was in the majority, and never will be for many a year to come. You may rest assured that if we were to poll the world for any opinion, and if that opinion should be decided by a majority, it would be necessarily wrong. Now and then in one country the right prevails, but all the world over the seed of the serpent outnumber the seed of the woman. Blessed is he who can stand in a minority of one with God; for a minority of one for God is in the judgment of truth a majority. Count God with you, and you have more with you than all they that be against you.

Fear and Temporal Things

I must not keep you much longer, for the heat grows great, and I fear some of you are fainting. Therefore I want to say another word which I should like you all to hear. This the fifth "Fear not." You will find it in Luke 12:32. Christ preaching to his disciples said,

"Fear not, little flock: for it is your Father's good pleasure to give you the kingdom."

This is meant to prevent fear as to temporal things. Now, I know that this is a time in which many of God's people are much tried, and they tremble lest they should not be provided for. Hearken to this: Did you escape from poverty by being frightened about it? Did your fears ever make you any the richer? Have you not found it to be vain to rise up early and to sit up late, and to eat the bread of carefulness when you have had no faith in God? Have you not learned that? And do you not know that if you are a child of God he will certainly give you your food and raiment? Ah, I hear a heavy sigh from one, "It has been a hard winter." It is true, my friend, it has been a hard winter. I dare say that the birds have found it so, and yet on Sunday morning I noticed when I opened my window early that they were singing very sweetly; and this morning, too, they broke forth in a chorus of harmonious song. You know what the little bird sings when he sits on a bare bough with the snow all around him? He chirps out—

> "Mortal, cease from toil and sorrow,
> God provideth for the morrow."

Learn the sparrow's song, and try, if you can, to catch the spirit of the bird which has no barn or storehouse, and yet is fed. There is this to comfort you: "Your heavenly Father knoweth what things ye have need of." He understands your wants. Is it not enough for a child that his father knows his needs? Rest in that, and be confident that verily you shall be fed. You will not have much in this world, perhaps; but you shall have the kingdom. Be of good cheer about that. Your inheritance is yet to come; you shall have the kingdom. You have even now a reversionary interest in eternal glory, and this involves present supplies: he who promises the end will provide for the way.

Some of the Lord's best people are those who have to suffer most, but it is because they can here glorify him most by suffering. I think the angels in heaven must almost envy a child of God who has the power and the privilege to suffer for Christ's sake; for doubtless angels render perfect service to the heavenly King, yet not by suffering. Theirs is active and not passive obedience to the will of God. Methinks they will cluster round some of you in heaven, and say, "You lived down at Bethnal Green, or Shoreditch. Ah, yes." The angels will say, "What sort of a place did you live in? One dark room? You were very poor: you were out of work: and did you trust God?" The angels will be pleased as you tell them, "O yes, we went to the heavenly Father still, and we said, 'Though he slay me, yet will I trust in him.'" That is the grandest thing that a man ever did say; at least, I think it is. Mr. Cuff says some fine things, but he never uttered a nobler sentence than that, "Though he slay me, yet will I trust in him." The expression is sublime! When Job had lost everything, after being immensely rich, he sat on a dunghill, and scraped his sores, and he said, "Naked came I out of my mother's womb, and naked shall I return thither." He was reduced to the most abject want, and yet he added—"The Lord gave, and the Lord hath taken away; blessed be the name of the Lord." Ye cherubim and seraphim, in all your songs no stanza excels that heroic verse. Angels cannot rise to such a height of sublime devotion to the Invisible One as Job did when in his misery he glorified his God by abiding confidence. Oh, you who are brought very low, you have grand opportunities for honoring God if you will but trust him. "Fear not." "Fear not."

> "Fear not the loss of outward good,
> He will for his provide,
> Give them supplies of daily food,
> And all they want beside."

And he will give you spiritual food too. When God saves his people he gives them spiritual food to live upon till they get to heaven. God does not give us treatment like that which the Duke of Alva measured out to a city which had surrendered. He agreed to give the inhabitants their lives, but when they complained that they were dying of hunger he maliciously replied, "I granted you your lives, but I did not promise you food." Our God does not talk so. He includes in the promise of salvation all that goes with it; and you shall have all you really want between here and heaven, wherefore fear not.

Fear and the Future

Lastly, time fails me: but I was going to close with that word in Acts 27:24, where the Lord sent his angel to his servant Paul in the time of the shipwreck, and said to him,

"Fear not, Paul; thou must be brought before Caesar: and lo, God hath given thee all them that sail with thee."

So I pray God that all perils in the future—all imminent ills and dangers which surround you now—may not cause you to fear, for the Lord will not suffer a hair of your head to perish, but he that has made you will bear you through, and make you more than conquerors too.

Tried people of God, rest in the Lord, and your confidence shall be your strength. You have often heard of the boy on board ship in time of storm who was the only person not afraid. When they asked him why he did not fear, he said, "Because my father is at the helm." We have still better cause for casting away all fear, for not only is our Father at the helm but our Father is everywhere, holding the winds and the waves in the hollow of his hand. No trouble can happen to you or to me but what he ordains or permits. No trial can come but what he will restrain and overrule. No evil can happen but what shall certainly work for good to them that love God. Therefore be not afraid. What though the howling tempest yell, and the ship creak and groan as she labors among the waves, and you think that nothing but destruction awaits you, fear not! Let not fear linger for a single moment in the presence of the eternal Christ who says, "It is I. Be not afraid." May God grant that his own "Fear not" may go home to the heart of everyone here present in some form or other; and unto his name be glory, world without end. Amen.

NOTES

NOTES

NOTES

The Conquest of Fear

George W. Truett (1867-1944) pastored the First Baptist Church of Dallas, Texas, from 1897 until his death, and saw it become the largest Southern Baptist Church in the world. He was a strong man with a tender heart, and undoubtedly he was one of the greatest preachers of his time. A devoted denominational leader, he served as president of the Southern Baptist Convention and the Baptist World Alliance. This sermon was taken from *Follow Thou Me* published in 1932 by the Broadman Press, Nashville.

George W. Truett

8

THE CONQUEST OF FEAR

Fear not; I am the first and the last, and the Living One; I
was dead, and behold, I am alive forevermore, and I have
the keys of death and of Hades (Revelation 1:17, 18).

IN THIS HOUR of worship, let us think together on Jesus'
greatest saying concerning the conquest of fear. It is given
in these words in the first chapter of the last book of the
New Testament. "Fear not; I am the first and the last,
and the Living One; I was dead, and behold, I am alive
forevermore, and I have the keys of death and of Hades."

It is both the mission and the message of Jesus to
deliver mankind from servile, enervating, down-dragging
fear. And certainly the problem of fear is a problem to be
reckoned with in many lives. One of the most outstanding
and surprising disclosures of our stressful, nervous, modern
civilization, is the fact that many people are ruled by fear.
This fact obtains with all classes of people—the high and
the low, the rich and the poor, the educated and ignorant,
the old and the young, with all ages and classes. They
have fears of all kinds—fear of themselves, of others, of
the past, present and future, of sickness, of death, of
poverty, and on and on.

A little while ago, it was my privilege to preach twice
daily for a week to one of our most influential American
colleges. Its student body is large and widely influential,
and more mature in years than is the student body of
most of our colleges. Before my arrival there, the president
of the college sent a questionnaire to every student, asking
that the students indicate any subjects upon which they
would have the visiting minister speak. When the answers
were tabulated, the president and faculty of the college,
together with the visiting minister and others, were
amazed by the fact that the majority of that large and

101

mature student body had made this request: "Let the visiting minister tell us how we may conquer fear."

Fear Not!

The Bible is the one book which answers that very question. There are two words which stand out in the Bible like mountain peaks—the words *Fear not!* With those words, God comforted Abraham, "Fear not, Abram; I am thy shield and exceeding great reward." With those same words he comforted Isaac at his lonely task of digging wells in the wilderness. With the same words he comforted Jacob, when his little Joseph was lost somewhere down in Egypt. So comforted he the Israelites at the Red Sea, "And Moses said unto the people, fear ye not, stand still and see the salvation of the Lord, which he will show you today." These two words, *Fear not!* standing out here and there in the Bible, are a part of our great inheritance as Christians. We shall do well to note them very carefully, wherever they occur in the Bible, and to note their contextual relations.

The three supreme matters which concern mankind are life, death and eternity. Jesus here gives us an all-comprehensive statement concerning these three vast matters. He bids us to be unafraid of life, of death and of eternity. It is Jesus' greatest saying concerning the conquest of fear. It was spoken to John, who was banished to Patmos because of his fealty to Christ. Let us now earnestly summon ourselves to think on this vast message of Jesus.

Do Not Fear Life

And first, Jesus bids us to be unafraid of life. He reminds us that he is "the first and the last and the Living One." Is the fear of life real? It is poignantly so with many. The liability of fear is constant, and this fact is perhaps the explanation for many a suicide. I asked one who sought in a despondent hour to snuff out the candle of life, and was prevented from so doing, "Why did you wish to end your life?" And the pathetic answer was given, "I was afraid to go on with life." People are afraid, for one thing, because they are so dependent. They are utterly dependent upon God, and greatly dependent upon one another.

Sometimes the proud expression is heard, "I am independent." Let such a one tell us of whom he is independent, and how and where and when. We are all bound together in the bundle of life. "For none of us liveth to himself, and no man dieth to himself."

Again, we are afraid because we are continually in the presence of great mysteries, such as the mystery of sin, of sorrow, of God, of one's own personality, and of the strange and ofttimes trying providences that come to us in the earthly life.

Still again, the responsibilities of life are such that serious men and women must often tremble. Piercing questions arise to probe our hearts to the depths. Often do we ask, "Will I make good in the stern battle of life?" "Will I disappoint the expectations of my loved ones and friends?" Even Moses trembled before his mighty responsibilities, thus voicing his fear, "O my Lord, I am not eloquent, neither heretofore, nor since thou hast spoken unto thy servant: but I am slow of speech, and of a slow tongue." And even Solomon shrank before his vast responsibility, saying, "And now, O Lord my God, thou hast made thy servant king instead of David my father; and I am but a little child: I know not how to go out or come in." Often come the testing hours in life, when we cry out with Paul, "Who is sufficient for these things?" Many times are we provoked to ask that very question, as we are called upon to make important decisions and meet the critically testing experiences of life. Verily, we are many times made to tremble before the immeasurably responsible facts of life. Jesus graciously comes to us, saying, "Do not be afraid of life." "I will never leave thee nor forsake thee."

Do Not Fear Death

Again, he bids us be unafraid of death. He reminds us, "I was dead, and behold, I am alive forevermore." The shuddering fear of death is a very real fact in many a life. Some are in bondage all their earthly lifetime, through fear of death. Maeterlinck confesses in his autobiography, "I am a frightened child in the presence of death." It is not to be wondered at that the thought of death casts its oppressive shadows about us, because death is an experience utterly strange to every one of us. "It is a borne whence no traveler returns." "The black camel kneels at every gate." "With equal pace, impartial fate knocks at the palace and the cottage gate."

It is not surprising that numbers of people have a strange fascination for prying into the secrets of death. This gruesome curiosity sometimes leads its possessor into strange quests and still stranger claims. What shall be said of these uncanny efforts to pry into the secrets of the dead? Such efforts are both profitless and presumptuous. Jesus has told us all that we need to know about death. He knows all about the grave, for he has explored its every chamber, and he has met this Waterloo of death and won. He is not now in the grave. He is alive, he is the Living One who is now bringing to bear the resources of his wisdom, mercy, power and love upon our needy world, and his will is bound to prevail. We are told that "ideas rule the world." Very well, compare the ideas proclaimed by Jesus with all others, and at once we see how preeminent his ideas are. The hands on his clock never turn backward. "For he must reign, till he hath put all enemies under his feet." Some day, thank God, war will be under his feet forever. And so will be all forms of intemperance, and selfishness and sin. And so will be death itself, because it is divinely decreed that "the last enemy that shall be destroyed is death." "O death, where is thy sting? O grave, where is thy victory? . . . But thanks be to God who giveth us the victory through our Lord Jesus Christ."

And still further—Jesus is with his people when they come to die. The evidences of this fact are countless and glorious. Often and joyfully did John Wesley declare, "Our people die well." Many of us, even in our limited and very humble sphere, can give the same glad testimony. "Our people die well." Indeed, when we see how well they can die, how unafraid and triumphant they are when they face the last enemy, we are fortified afresh for our work of testifying to the sufficiency of Christ's help in every possible human experience.

Not long ago, I saw a timid mother die. Hers was a very humble home, the husband was a carpenter, the children were very modestly clothed, and the limitations imposed by a meager income for the home were markedly in evidence. With a calmness, fearlessness and joyfulness indescribable, that modest woman faced the final chapter of the earthly journey. She gave her sublime Christian testimony to her sorrowing husband and children; she confidently bound them to the heart of God, in a prayer that can never be forgotten by those who heard it; and then she passed into the valley of the shadows, smilingly whispering the victorious words, "Yea, though I walk though the valley of the shadow of death, I will fear no evil, for thou art with me; thy rod and thy staff they comfort me."

The next day, I saw a strong husband and father pass to the great beyond. He requested that the pastor pray that the whole household might unreservedly accept God's will. When the prayer was concluded, the strong man who was rapidly hurrying down to death sublimely said to the poignantly sorrowing wife and sons, "This is God's way; he doeth all things well; I accept his will without a question; tell me, O my dear wife and children, will you not likewise accept his will in this hour, and through all the unfolding future?" And with one voice, they said, "We will." And then, the strong man was gone, and the peace and calm of Heaven filled all that house.

A third day came, and I was called to witness the passing of an unusually timid girl in the Sunday school. The modest child of little more than a dozen years of age anxiously said to her mother, "Everything is getting dark, Mamma. Come close to me, I'm afraid." And the gentle mother said to the little daughter, "Jesus is with us in the dark, my child, as well as in the light, and he will surely take care of all who put their trust in him." And the child's face was immediately lighted up with a joyful smile, as she said, "I am trusting him, and I'll just keep on trusting him, and he will stay close to me, for he said he would, and he always does what he says he will do." And a little later, even in life's closing moments, her voice could be heard singing, "There'll be no dark valley when Jesus comes to gather his children home."

Such illustrations of triumph in the hour of death could be indefinitely multiplied. The pastors of your churches are privileged to witness such triumphs week by week; and they are able, therefore, to stand in their pulpits and victoriously shout with Paul, "But thanks be to God, who giveth us the victory through our Lord Jesus Christ."

Do Not Fear Eternity

Not only does Jesus bid us be unafraid of life and of death, but he also bids us to be unafraid of eternity. The word he speaks here in his great promise is, "I have the keys of death and of Hades." That little word "keys" carries with it a large meaning. It means guidance, it means authority, it means control. Just as Jesus cares for his people in life and in death, even so will he care for them in eternity. "I go to prepare a place for you. And if I go and prepare a place for you, I will come again, and receive you unto myself; that where I am, there ye may be also."

Belief in God and in immortality go together. The age-old question, "If a man die, shall he live again?" is a question that will not be hushed. It is no wonder that such a question has been eagerly asked by myriads in recent years. The Great War laid millions of young men under sod and sea, and has sent other millions to stagger on with broken health, even down to the grave. Suffering hearts all around the encircling globe have asked and are continually asking if death is an eternal sleep, and if the grave ends all. To such questions we must give our most positive answer. The grave does not end all. The doctrine of immortality is not a dead creed, an empty speculation, an intellectual curiosity, an interesting question. The doctrine of immortality is a fact, a force, a great moral dynamic, which lifts life to high levels and drives it to great ends. Yes, we are to live again, beyond the sunset and the night, to live on consciously, personally and forever.

The nature of man demands immortality. The instinct of immortality is the prophecy of its fulfillment. Where in all nature can you find instinct falsified? The wings of the bird mean that it was made to fly. The fins of the fish mean that it was made to swim. The deathless yearnings of the heart imperiously cry out for immortality. On the modest monument that marks the last resting place in France of President Roosevelt's son, who fell in the Great War, is inscribed this death-defying sentence, "He has outsoared the shadow of our night." The human heart refuses to be hushed in its cry for immortality.

The character of God presages immortality. When Job thought of men, he said, "If a man die, shall he live again?" When he thought of God, he said, "I know that my Redeemer liveth." Then Job went on to voice the deathless cry of the heart for immortality. God is infinitely interested in us, he cares for us, he provides for us. If he cares for the birds, as he does, surely he cares also for us. He bids us to put fear away, reminding us, "But the very hairs of your head are all numbered." "Fear ye not, therefore, ye are of more value than many sparrows." Abraham was "the friend of God." Death has not dissolved that friendship.

"Enoch walked with God; and he was not, for God took him." A little girl who heard a preacher's sermon on this sentence gave this report of the sermon to a little neighbor girl who did not hear the sermon, "The preacher said that Enoch took a long walk with God; and they walked, and they walked, and they walked; and at last, God told Enoch that he need not go back to live at his house anymore, but he could just go on home with God, to live with him, in his house, forever." Surely, the little girl's interpretation is what our hearts demand, and it is what we steadfastly and joyfully believe to be the plan of God for his friends.

But the crowning argument for immortality is the experience of Jesus. He has incontestably proved it. He came to earth, and really lived, and died, and was buried, and rose again, just as he said he would do. Long years ago, the men of the Old World wondered if there was some other land, beyond the waters, to the far west. One day, a bolder spirit than others had been set sail toward the west. And by and by, Columbus set his feet upon the shores of a new land.

Even so, Jesus was the divine Columbus who has explored all the chambers of the grave, and has come back therefrom, the victorious Conqueror of death. He comforts his friends with the gracious words, "I am the resurrection and the life; he that believeth in me, though he were dead, yet shall he live. And whosoever liveth and believeth in me shall never die." In that incomparable chapter of guidance and comfort, the fourteenth chapter of John, Jesus would anchor us, once for all, with his divinely assuring words, "Because I live, ye shall live also."

> Low in the grave He lay—Jesus my Savior!
> Waiting the coming day, Jesus my Lord!
> Up from the grave, He arose,
> With a mighty triumph o'er His fores;
> He arose a Victor from the dark domain,
> And He lives forever, with His saints to reign,
> He arose! He arose! Hallelujah! Christ arose!

With our faith in that victorious Savior, we may sing with Whittier, in his exquisite poem, "Snowbound."

> Alas for him who never sees
> The stars shine through his cypress trees!
> Who, hopeless, lays his dead away,
> Nor looks to see the breaking day,
> Across the mournful marbles play!
> Who hath not learned, in hours of faith,
> The truth to flesh and sense unknown,
> That Life is ever lord of Death,
> And Love can never lose its own!

Are you trusting in Christ as your personal Savior, and do you gladly bow to him as your rightful Master? If your hearts answer "Yes," go your many scattered ways, I pray you, without hesitation or fear. Your personal relations to Christ will determine your relations to the three vast matters—life, death and eternity—concerning which he would have us put all our fears away, now and forever more. He is our Pilot, our Righteousness, our Savior, our

Advocate, our promised and infallible Guide, even unto death, and throughout the vast beyond, forever. Well do we often sing, "He leadeth me." As we sing it now, who wishes openly to confess him and follow him?

NOTES

NOTES

Under His Wings

John Henry Jowett (1864-1923) was known as "the greatest preacher in the English-speaking world." Born in Yorkshire, England, he was ordained into the Congregational ministry. His second pastorate was at the famous Carr's Lane Church, Birmingham, where he followed the eminent Dr. Robert W. Dale. From 1911-18, he pastored the Fifth Avenue Presbyterian Church, New York City; and from 1918-23, he ministered at Westminster Chapel, London, succeeding G. Campbell Morgan. He wrote many books of devotional messages and sermons. This message comes from *Apostolic Optimism*, published in 1930 by Richard R. Smith, Inc., New York.

John Henry Jowett

9

UNDER HIS WINGS

He shall cover thee with His feathers, and under His wings shalt thou trust: His truth shall be thy shield and buckler. Thou shalt not be afraid for the terror by night, nor for the arrow that flieth by day, nor for the pestilence that walketh in darkness, nor for the destruction that wasteth at noonday (Psalm 91:4-6).

"THE TERROR BY NIGHT!" "The arrow that flieth by day!" "The pestilence that walketh in darkness!" "The destruction that wasteth at noonday!" What an appalling catalog of foes! They are not peculiar to any one life; they haunt the precincts of all lives. They pervade all the changing hours and moods of the varied day. Every change in the day's march reveals a special and characteristic foe. If life is passing through the season of midnight blackness, it is exposed to the antagonism of the "terror by night." If life has emerged from the blackness, and is passing out into the sweet and broadening light, it becomes endangered by "the arrow that flieth by day." If life is luxuriating under the cloudless, glowing sky of a wealthy noontide, it is imperiled by "the destruction that wasteth at noonday." If the shadows are gathering round again, and the light is fading from the sky, and life experiences the chill of the looming night, it may become the victim of "the pestilence that walketh in darkness." In one or other of these changing seasons we may probably all be found. There is an enemy about us in the noontide, and another in the midnight, and other foes inhabit the twilights of evening and dawn. Let us look a little while at these insidious enemies which beset the child of God.

The Terror by Night

There are many things which become terrific and terrifying through the medium of the night. In the night-

113

time faint sounds become laden with alarming significance. The creaking of the furniture in the room is almost suggestive of the opening of coffins. The stirring of the window by the moving night-air is suggestive of unfriendly approach. The scratching of a mouse at the wainscot becomes fraught with all manner of hostile invasion. As it is with the hearing, so is it with the sight. Vague outlines are filled out into portentous completeness. A bramble-bush represents itself as a crouching foe. A patch of snow in the corner of the field images itself as a sheeted ghost. "Things are not what they seem." In the night we are the victims of exaggeration. The commonplace becomes aggravated. The molehill becomes a mountain. Is not this equally true of the life of the Spirit? How everything rears itself into calamitous proportions when we are "down"! How the petty obstacles become enlarged and multiplied! We see things out of their proportions. We lose the calmness and clearness of our discernment. This is assuredly part of the enemy's forces, who is known as "the terror by night."

The Arrow That Flieth by Day

The night is past; the sweet fresh daylight is spread over the life; the terror born of exaggeration is forgotten. Is there no other foe? Enemies may be begotten of sunbeams as well as of darkness. The rays of light may become the arrows of death. How often it happens when men come into the clear happy light of favor, some better part of their being is slain! I wonder how many Sunday school teachers there are in the land with incomes at the poverty level! It is a most significant question. How is it that our Sunday schools are staffed with comparatively poor men and women? You hear it said of one man, "Oh, he has lost interest in that now." Lost? That sounds like something slain. He has been pierced by "the arrow that flieth by day," and some holy sympathy has been destroyed. Or an arrow has transfixed his geniality, his spirit of good-fellowship, and the winsome thing lies dead. He may have been saved from the "terror by night"; he has become the victim of the "arrow that flieth by day."

The Destruction That Wasteth at Noonday

This only marks the emphasis of the dangers of the brightening day. It proclaims the perils of the cloudless noon. A frosty night can harden the land, and make it impervious to the ministry of the farmer, but the fierce sunshine can attain the same end. Winter can freeze the land until it is as hard as iron; a succession of June noontides can bake it quite as hard. Adversity can dry up a man's sympathies; prosperity can induce as severe a drought. When a man's life passes into the full blaze of a fierce prosperity, the bloom and beauty of his spirit may be easily wasted and destroyed. His leaf may wither. His reverence may be destroyed. His aspirations may be dried up. Pride may supplant the grace of lowliness, and cocksureness may jostle out the spirit of "a quiet walk with God."

The Pestilence That Walketh in Darkness

When the brightness of the afternoon begins to grow dim in the shadows of coming night, and a chill air touches the happy and comfortable spirit, there is great danger of the life becoming possessed by "the pestilence that walketh in darkness." It is not easy to keep a room sweet which is deprived of the sunlight. Fustiness begins to reign where the light is not a guest. We need the help of the Almighty to keep the life sweet when the sunshine is temporarily withdrawn. Everybody knows the ill plagues that stir about us when life comes into the shadows. There is the pestilence of fretfulness, and melancholy, and murmuring, and despair. The heart is sorely prone when it first encounters the chilly shadows of an unexpected night.

Not let us turn away from the foes, and contemplate our resources. We have looked at the enemies; now let us look at our all-sufficient Friend.

He Shall Cover Thee With His Feathers

Against all possible types of enemies we may enjoy the protection of the great Mother-Bird, God. "He shall *cover* thee." The protection is to be perfectly complete. The wings would enfold us so that there is no possible opening for the dangerous approach of a foe. What may we not hope to gain in such a gracious refuge? We may expect to find *healing*. "The Sun of Righteousness shall arise with healing in His wings." If we have been wounded by the arrow, or affrighted by the terrors of the night, we shall be healed and comforted under the shadow of the Almighty. The troubled, frightened child, who has been startled in the darkness of the night, is hugged to its mother's breast, and speedily the panting, agitated little heart is comforted into rest again. And if we have been seeing things, and hearing things, out of their true shapes and proportions, the comforting breast of our God will restore us to quietness again. "Let not your heart be troubled." Let it not be agitated and alarmed. "Come unto Me, and I will give you rest."

And if we may gain healing, we shall also surely gain *security*. In an old Puritan writer I have found the phrase, "Under His wings we have curing and securing." The quaint expression serves my purpose tonight. Under the wings of the Almighty our wounds are healed, and our alarms are stilled, and a joyful confidence pervades the soul. We may be in the night, but no terror will disturb us. We may be in the broadening light, but no arrow will wound us. We may be in the noontide, but no glare will consume us. We may be in the shadows, but no pestilence will corrupt us. "Under His wings will I take refuge."

His Truth Shall Be Thy Shield and Buckler

The Psalmist is implying a variety of figures that he may make clear to us the amplitude of the protecting grace of God. He is not contented with the wealthy figure of the Mother-Bird; he adds another—"Thy shield." And then, as if both figures were not sufficiently emphatic and effective, he adds a third—"Thy buckler." The shield may appear to be only a partial defense, but the buckler is an all-surrounding coat of mail, covering the person on every side. There is no part left exposed to the enemy's attack. Before and behind, on the right hand and on the left, I am beset by the protective power of God. To what does the Psalmist attribute this mighty defense? "His truth." "His truth shall be thy Shield and Buckler."

Perhaps we may express the pith of the Psalmist's meaning by using in place of the word "truth" the more personal word "truthfulness," or "trustworthiness." Mark, then, this: it is not our feelings which are to be our defense. Our feelings may be as changeable as a barometer, and building upon them we have no fixed, dependable resource. If I am to judge the defenses of my religious life by the state and quality of my feelings, then I can clearly see that there are breaches in the wall every day, through which the evil one may make his attack. I turn from my feelings to the truthfulness of God. At once I pass from loose stones to compact rock. His truthfulness, the sure word of His promise, is to be my strong defense. "Hath He not said, and shall He not do it?" What has He said about your past? "Shall He not do it?" What has He said about your present? "Shall He not do it?" What has He said concerning your tomorrow? "Shall He not do it?" "His truth shall be thy shield and buckler."

Thou Shalt Not Be Afraid

Hiding beneath His wings, and depending upon the sure word of His promise, "thou shalt not be afraid." Thy life shall be possessed by a fruitful quietness. Thou shalt reap "the harvest of a quiet eye." Every changing mood of the varied day shall bring thee good and not ill. The night-time shall bring its treasure. The morning shall be the minister of gracious dews. The noonday shall deposit its glory, "and at evening time it shall be light."

NOTES

NOTES

The Courage of Consecration

Hugh Black (1868-1953) was born and trained in Scotland and ministered with Alexander Whyte at Free St. George's in Edinburgh. He served as professor of Homiletics at Union Theological Seminary, New York (1906-1938), and was widely recognized as a capable preacher. This sermon is taken from *Listening to God* by Hugh Black, published in 1906 by Fleming H. Revell.

Hugh Black

10

THE COURAGE OF CONSECRATION

And I said, should such a man as I flee (Nehemiah 6:11)?

THE MEMOIRS OF Nehemiah present to us a record of noble endeavor, and show us what can be achieved by one man of courage and faith, whose life is ruled by unswerving allegiance to duty. They reveal Nehemiah as a man of deep feeling and tireless energy and stern resolution. He has his place in the history of revelation, not because of any profound thought on the problems of life, nor because of new insight into truth, but because of what he was enabled to do at a critical period of Israel's history. He was not a prophet who saw visions, nor a poet who interpreted the heart of man. He has no place in the long line of thinkers who have opened up new regions for the human spirit. He was rather a man of affairs, keen, practical, with genius for organization, a born leader of men, a man of iron nerve and passionate energy. He was the typical statesman in a day of small things, rather than the typical prophet like Isaiah, who was a statesman also, but with larger vision and dealing with wider interests. He was a practical business man throwing his great capacities into work for the good of his nation.

In a time like ours, when such qualities stand so high in public estimation, and among a people like us more noted for energy than for thought, for business than for vision, it is encouraging to note how similar capacities were in Nehemiah's case used for the Kingdom of Heaven. All the powers that dwell within a man can find ample scope, if they be only set to noble ends. Nothing is common and unclean among man's gifts if it be not consecrated.

The Church will not take her rightful place and perform her perfect work, until she can command these qualities so common in our midst, until men realize that they are called to give of all they have to her service. Enthusiasm for social progress, business talent, power of organization, capacity to deal with practical affairs, even financial genius, all those very attributes most highly developed today, should be offered in greater degree than they are. Men who possess them are as much bound to devote them to larger ends than merely selfish ones, as men endowed with the rarer gifts of brain and heart. This is surely one great lesson from the life of Nehemiah. But for the consecration of these very gifts he would have been nothing but a successful man of affairs, or a high-placed permanent official, or a skillful counselor at the Persian court. Because in the power of a simple faith he gave himself to a great work, he stands in the succession of prophets and psalmists and saints and apostles, having spent himself for the Kingdom of God. Can any personal success compare with taking a share in the coming of the Kingdom? We need a higher conception of service, the consecration of all gifts to the service of God and men. Without this it will be to find at the last that you have spent your strength for naught and have given your labor for vanity.

Courage in the Face of Difficulty

Another lesson from Nehemiah's example is the lesson of courage that will not be daunted by difficulties, resolution to adhere to the path of duty, let come what may. The incident to which our text refers is an illustration of this. The task to which Nehemiah set himself was one, he soon discovered, which demanded all his energy and perseverance. Surrounded by the hostility of implacable foes of Jerusalem, who would stick at no treachery to prevent the fulfillment of his purposes, he had to fan the flickering flame of patriotism within his own countrymen. The enmity outside was no greater than the feebleness and cowardice within. A less stouthearted man would have given up in despair, when he learned to what lengths of treachery his opponents were prepared to go. Cajolements, threats, charges of conspiracy against the King of Persia, open violence and covert attack, were all hurled at him, and all failed to make him even stop the work for a moment. He only said, "O God, strengthen my hands," as he drove on with his great task of building the walls of the city and securing it against attack.

Even the word of a prophet was perverted to force him to desist. Shemaiah pretended to reveal a plot formed against him, and as if in terror for him and for himself, besought him to take refuge in the Temple. "Let us go together to the house of God within the Temple; for they will come to slay thee; yea, in the night will they come to slay thee." It was a mean plan to compass Nehemiah's ruin in another way—to make him ruin himself. It was the height of impiety for a man who was not a priest to trespass in the Temple; and for the governor to do this to save his life would have alienated from him the sympathy of all the best people in the city, all the pious Jews who were his chief supporters. Shemaiah's veiled argument is that the safety of such an important life as that of the governor was of more value than the punctilious keeping of a Temple law.

The force of the temptation to a religious man like Nehemiah was that the advice came to him through the mouth of a prophet. It seemed as if God commanded him to follow it. But he judged the counsel by his own moral sense and perceived that it was false; for God could not ask him at once to neglect his plain duty and at the same time commit a sin against the ceremonial law. He saw that the prophet was hired by his enemies to frighten him and compel him to do what would be accounted a sin, and thus have matter for an evil report to undermine his influence and achieve their own base designs. His answer was in keeping with his own resolute life. "Should such a man as I flee? Who is there that being such as I would go into the Temple to save his life? I will not go in." If need be he would die at his post. Not even to escape assassination could he, the leader of the great enterprise, show the white feather. The place of duty might be a place of danger, but he dare not flinch from it on that account. Humanly speaking, everything depended on him; and for him to weaken and desert even to save his life would be to ruin the cause. Instead of the fact of his being governor being an excuse for considering his own safety, it was the very opposite. Just because he was in a position of responsibility with every eye on him, and because there lay on him a heavy burden of duty, he must be true even though it should mean death. "Should such a man as I flee?"

The Courage of Faith

The courage which Nehemiah displayed was the courage of faith. He felt himself called to do this work, and he would do it at any cost. He believed that God was with him, and he was not going to turn tail and flee at the first sign of danger. There is a courage which is common enough, the courage of hot blood, which is a sort of animal instinct. It seems even constitutional in some races. This physical courage is only what we expect in men of our breed, an inheritance from our ancestors. We so seldom see past the surface that we often mistake the very qualities which compose the highest kind of courage. We praise a man because we say he does not know fear; but this may be mere insensibility. Some courage is due to want of thought, or want of imagination, or want of care for others. It may be only a dare-devil recklessness. But true courage needs to have something more in it than this quality of hot blood.

Dumas in his great character of D'Artagnan, whom he meant to be the typical brave soldier, gives a touch which shows how real courage implies sensitive feeling mastered by a strong will. "D'Artagnan, thanks to his ever-active imagination, was afraid of a shadow; and ashamed of being afraid, he marched straight up to that shadow, and then became extravagant in his bravery if the danger proved to be real." Even physical courage is not simply absence of fear, not simply thoughtless, heedless daring. It needs to be related to a moral quality before it can take any high place as a virtue.

This true courage is rather steadfastness of mind, the calm, resolute fixity of purpose which holds to duty in the scorn of consequence. Nehemiah displayed this kind of courage when, alive to the presence of danger, knowing well the risk and counting all the cost, he turned upon the tempter with the indignant question, "Should such a man as I flee?" He stood in the path of duty, and therefore in the very line of God's will, and he would not budge one inch. Luther showed the same courage when the Elector wrote to him before the Diet of Worms reminding him that John Huss had been burnt at the Council of Constance, although he also possessed a safe-conduct. Luther replied that he would go to Worms if there were as many devils there as tiles on the roofs. He knew well that the chances were that he was going to his death; but he also knew that he was obeying conscience and obeying the truth by going. To his dear friend Melanchthon, who was in distress at their parting, he said, "My dear brother, if I do not come back, if my enemies put me to death, you will go on teaching and standing fast in the truth: if *you* live, *my* death will matter little." He too, like Nehemiah, was sustained by the thought of duty, by the sense of responsibility as the leader of a great movement, and by a resolute faith in God. "Should such a man as I flee?"

Moral Courage

There is no quality more necessary for noble living than this moral courage; and there is no quality the lack of which is responsible for more failures. Courage of a sort is common enough, but this courage is rare, this steadfastness of heart, this unmovable adherence to duty, which turns an obstinate face to temptation, whether it come in the form of allurement or in the form of threat. Yet without it a strong character cannot possibly be formed. What examples we are of weakness of will, infirmity of purpose, instability of life, indecision of character. We need more iron in our blood. We need to have our natures hardened to withstand. Young men and women need to think a little less of pleasure and a little more of duty. We give in to every dominant impulse through sheer moral cowardice and feebleness of mind.

In its essence great courage like Nehemiah's is great faith. It was because he believed in God, and believed that he was doing God's will, that he was able to rise above all selfish fears. This is the secret of strength. As the Psalmist said, "I have set the Lord always before me; because He is at my right hand, I shall not be moved." Well might Nehemiah be strong and of a good courage when he felt himself within the sweep of God's purpose, when he had emptied his heart of all selfish desires and sought only to do God's will. Well might he say, Should such a man as I flee?—a man sure of himself because sure of God, a man privileged to undertake a great work, a man who feels himself a co-worker with God for the high ends of His Kingdom. It is only the same cause that can produce the same effect. If we had the same simple confidence in God, the same submission to His will, the same consecration of all our powers, we would have something of the same calm courage. If we made more of duty, and took the burden humbly on our shoulders, we would be strengthened by the very bearing of the burden to endure it. Faith is the true method of life, after all. Courage is the true way to high success. A sense of duty to God will save a man from weakness, will breed in him the iron nerve and steadfast courage and the endurance which is the crowning quality of great hearts.

> Not once or twice in our rough island story
> The path of duty was the way to glory.

And if the path of duty be not to all the way to glory in the large pubic sense in which Tennyson used these words about the Duke of Wellington, it will be at least the way to peace and true honor. Unless there be in a man's life a sense of duty which makes certain things necessary, things that he ought to do and must do, and certain things that he must refuse and will refuse at all costs, how can he escape being weak and wavering? He is the fit mark for any sudden and swift temptation. Unless a man can take his stand upon right and stiffen his neck against temptation to desert it, how can he expect to avoid open shame somewhere? Without it you are the victims, never the masters of your fate. Till you have some courage of conviction, refusing to follow even a multitude to do evil, till you know the bit and the bridle and the spur of duty,

going its way and not your own way, you are useless for
the world's best ends. Till you have learned to say No,
everlasting No, on some subjects; No, everlasting No, to
some enticements, you have not begun to live as a moral
being. There is nothing that our young men and women
need more today than this courage, which adds a hard
fiber to conscience, and gives stability to character. We
are too pliant and flexible and flabby, too easily cowed
into giving up principles, too easily moved by a sneer, too
easily browbeaten by a majority, too timid in following
our own best instincts. The sense of duty, paramount and
supreme, seems weakened in our midst.

Duty cannot be maintained as an inviolate rule of life
without moral courage; and courage cannot be maintained
without consecration. Thus it is religion which preserves
sacredness to human duty. It is the inspiring fount of
noble endeavor. When a man is consumed with the desire
to please God, he is long past the mere desire to please
self. When the heart is fixed, the feet naturally take the
path of God's commandments. The new affection moves
the life to new obedience. The love of Christ drives out the
lower loves; and gives power in the hour of temptation.
Should such a man as I, redeemed, sanctified, with the
seal on my brow and the cross on my heart, flee from my
corner of the battlefield?

NOTES

NOTES

Fear and Faith

Alexander Maclaren (1826-1910) was one of Great Britain's most famous preachers. While pastoring the Union Chapel, Manchester (1858-1903), he became known as "the prince of expository preachers." Rarely active in denominational or civic affairs, Maclaren invested his time studying the Word in the original and sharing its truths with others in sermons that are still models of effective expository preaching. He published a number of books of sermons and climaxed his ministry by publishing his monumental *Expositions of Holy Scripture*.

This message is taken from *Week-Day Evening Addresses*, published by Funk and Wagnalls Company (1902).

Alexander Maclaren

11

FEAR AND FAITH

What time I am afraid, I will trust in Thee. . . . In God
I have put my trust; I will not fear (Psalm 56:3, 4).

IT IS NOT given to many men to add new words to the
vocabulary of religious emotion. But so far as an
examination of the Old Testament avails, I find that David
was the first that ever employed the word that is here
translated, *I will trust*, with a religious meaning. It is
found occasionally in earlier books of the Bible in different
connections, never in regard to man's relations to God,
until the Poet-Psalmist laid his hand upon it, and
consecrated it for all generations to express one of the
deepest relations of man to his Father in heaven.

And it is a favorable word of his. I find it occurs
constantly in his psalms; twice as often, or nearly so, in
the psalms attributed to David as in all the rest of the
Psalter put together; and, as I shall have occasion to show
you in a moment, it is in itself a most significant and
poetic word.

The Occasion of Trust

But, first of all, I ask you to notice how beautifully
there comes out here the *occasion* of trust. "What time I
am afraid, I will put my trust in Thee."

This psalm is one of those belonging to the Sauline
persecution. If we adopt the allocation in the
superscription, it was written at one of the very lowest
points of his fortunes. And there seem to be one or two of
its phrases which acquire new force, if we regard the
psalm as drawn forth by the perils of his wandering,
hunted life. For instance—"Thou tellest my wanderings,"
is no mere expression of the feelings with which he
regarded the changes of this earthly pilgrimage, but is

131

the confidence of the fugitive that in the doublings and windings of his flight God's eye marked him. "Put thou my tears into Thy *bottle*"—one of the few indispensable articles which he had to carry with him, the water-skin which hung beside him, perhaps, as he meditated. So read in the light of his probable circumstances, how pathetic and eloquent does that saying become—"What time I am afraid, I will trust in Thee." That goes deep down into the realities of life. It is when we are "afraid" that we trust in God; not in easy times, when things are going smoothly with us. Not when the sun shines, but when the tempest blows and the wind howls about his ears, a man gathers his cloak round him, and cleaves fast to his supporter. The midnight sea lies all black; but when it is cut into by the oar, or divided and churned by the paddle, it flashes up into phosphorescence. And so it is from the tumults and agitation of man's spirit that there is struck out the light of man's faith. There is the bit of flint and the steel that comes hammering against it; and it is the contact of these two that brings out the spark. The man never knew confidence who does not know how the occasion that evoked and preceded was terror and need. "What time I am *afraid*, I will trust." That is no trust which is only fair weather trust. This principle— first fear, and only then, faith—applies all round the circle of our necessities, weaknesses, sorrows, and sins.

There must, first of all, be the deep sense of need, of exposedness to danger, of weakness, of sorrow, and only then will there come the calmness of confidence. A victorious faith will

> "—rise large and slow
> From out the fluctuations of our souls,
> As from the dim and tumbling sea
> Starts the completed moon."

And then, if so, notice how there is involved in that the other consideration, that a man's confidence is not the product of outward circumstances, but of his own fixed resolves. "I *will* put my trust in Thee."

Nature says, Be afraid, and the recoil from that natural

fear, which comes from a discernment of threatening evil, is only possible by a strong effort of the will. Foolish confidence opposes to natural fear a groundless resolve not to be afraid, as if heedlessness were security, or facts could be altered by resolving not to think about them. True faith, by a mighty effort of the will, fixes its gaze on our Divine helper, and there finds it possible and wise to lose its fears. It is madness to say, I will not be afraid; it is wisdom and peace to say, I will trust, and not be afraid. But it is no easy matter to fix the eye on God when threatening enemies within arm's length compel our gaze; and there must be a fixed resolve, not indeed to coerce our emotions or to ignore our perils, but to set the Lord before us, that we may not be moved. When war desolates a land, the peasants fly from their undefended huts to the shelter of the castle on the hill-top, but they cannot reach the safety of the strong walls without climbing the steep road. So when calamity darkens round us, or our sense of sin and sorrow shakes our hearts, we need effort to resolve and to carry into practice the resolution, "I flee unto Thee to hide me."

Fear, then, is the occasion of faith, and faith is fear transformed by the act of our own will, calling to mind the strength of God, and betaking ourselves thereto. Therefore, do not wonder if the two things lie in your hearts together, and do not say, "I have no faith because I have some fear," but rather feel that if there be the least spark of the former it will turn all the rest into its own bright substance.

Here is the stifling smoke, coming up from some newly-lighted fire of green wood, black and choking, and solid in its coils; but as the fire burns up, all the smoke-wreaths will be turned into one flaming spire, full of light and warmth. Do you turn your smoke into fire, your fear into faith. Do not be downhearted if it takes a while to convert the whole of the lower and baser into the nobler and higher. Faith and fear do blend, thank God. They are as oil and water in a man's soul, and the oil will float above, and quiet the waves. "What time I am afraid"—there speaks the better man within, lifting himself above nature and circumstances, and casting himself into the extended arms of God, who catches him and keeps him safe.

The Essence of Trust

Then, still further, these words, or rather one portion of them, give us a bright light and a beautiful thought as to the *essence* and inmost center of this faith or trust. Scholars tell us that the word here translated "trust" has a graphic, pictorial meaning for its root idea. It signifies literally to cling to or hold fast anything, expressing thus both the notion of a good tight grip and of intimate union. Now, is not that metaphor vivid and full of teaching as well as of impulse? "I will trust in Thee." "And he exhorted them all, that with purpose of heart they should *cleave* unto the Lord." We may follow out the metaphor of the word in many illustrations. For instance, here is a strong prop, and here is the trailing, lithe feebleness of the vine. Gather up the leaves that are creeping all along the ground, and coil them around that support, and up they go straight towards the heavens.

Here is a limpet in some pond or other, left by the tide, and it has relaxed its grasp a little. Touch it with your finger and it grips fast to the rock, and you will want a hammer before you can dislodge it. There is a traveler groping along some narrow broken path, where the chamois would tread cautiously, his guide in front of him. His head reels, and his limbs tremble, and he is all but over, but he grasps the strong hand of the man in front of him, or lashes himself to him by the rope, and he can walk steadily.

Or, take that story in the Acts of the Apostles, about the lame man healed by Peter and John. All his life long he had been lame, and when at last healing comes, one can fancy with what a tight grasp "the lame man held Peter and John." The timidity and helplessness of a life-time made him hold fast, even while, walking and leaping, he tried how the unaccustomed "feet and ankle bones" could do their work. How he would clutch the arms of his two supporters, and feel himself firm and safe only as long as he grasped them! That is faith, cleaving to Christ, twining round Him with all the tendrils of our heart, as the vine does round its pole; holding to Him by His hand, as a tottering man does by the strong hand that upholds.

And there is one more application of the metaphor, which perhaps may be best brought out by referring to a passage of Scripture. We find this same expression used in that wonderfully dramatic scene in the Book of Kings, where the supercilious messengers from the king of Assyria came up and taunted the king and his people on the wall. "What confidence is this wherein thou trustest? Now, on whom dost thou trust, that thou rebellest against me? Now, behold, thou trustest upon the staff of this bruised reed, even upon Egypt, on which, if a man lean, it will go into his hand and pierce it: so is Pharaoh, king of Egypt, unto all that trust on him."

The word of our text is employed there, and, as the phrase shows, with a distinct trace of its primary sense. You are trusting or leaning upon this poor paper reed on the Nile banks, that has no substance, or strength, or pith in it. A man leans upon it, and it runs into the palm of his hand, and makes an ugly festering wound. Such rotten stays are all our earthly confidences. The act of trust, and the miserable issues of placing it on man, are excellently described there. The act is the same when directed to God, but how different the issues. Lean all your weight on God as on some strong staff, and depend upon it that support will never yield nor crack; there will no splinters run into your palms for it.

If I am to cling with my hand I must first empty my hand. Fancy a man saying, I cannot stand unless you hold me up; but I have to hold my Bank Book, and this thing, and that thing, and the other thing; I cannot put them down, so I have not a hand free to lay hold with, you must do the holding. That is what some of us are saying in effect. Now the prayer, "Hold Thou me up, and I shall be safe," is a right one; but from a man who will not put his possessions out of his hands, that he may lay hold of the God who lays hold of him.

"Nothing in my hands I bring."

Then of course, and only then, when we are empty-handed, shall we be free to grip and lay hold; and only then shall we be able to go on with the grand words—

"Simply to Thy cross I cling."

Thus, some half-drowned, shipwrecked sailor, flung up on the beach, clasps a point of rock, and is safe from the power of the waves that beat around him.

The Victory of Faith

And then one word more. These two clauses that I have put together give us not only the occasion of faith in fear, and the essence of faith in this clinging, but they also give us very beautifully the *victory* of faith. You see with what poetic art—if we may use such words about the breathings of such a soul—he repeats the two main words of the former verse in the latter, only in inverted order—"What time I afraid, I will trust in Thee." He is possessed by the lower emotion, and resolves to escape from its sway into the light and liberty of faith. And then the next words still keep up the contrast of faith and fear, only that now he is possessed by the more blessed mood, and determines that he will not fall back into the bondage and darkness of the baser. "In God I have put my trust; I will not fear." He has confidence, and in the strength of this he resolves that he will not yield to fear. If we put that thought into a more abstract form it comes to this: that the one true antagonist and triumphant rival of all fear is faith, and faith alone. There is no reason why any man should be emancipated from his fears either about this world or about the next, except in proportions as he has faith. Nay, rather it is far away more rational to be afraid than not to be afraid, unless I have this faith in Christ. There are plenty of reasons for dread in the dark possibilities and not less dark certainties of life. Disasters, losses, partings, disappointments, sicknesses, death, may any of them come at any moment, and some of them will certainly come sooner or later.

Temptations lurk around us like serpents in the grass, they beset us in open ferocity like lions in our path. Is it not wise to fear unless our faith has hold of that great promise, "Thou shalt tread upon the lion and adder; there shall be no evil befall thee"? But if we have a firm hold of God, then it is wise not to be afraid, and terror is folly and sin. For trust brings not only tranquillity, but security, and so takes away fear by taking away danger.

That double operation of faith in quieting and in defending is very strikingly set forth by an Old Testament word, formed from the verb here employed, which means properly *confidence*, and then in one form comes to signify both *in security* and *in safety*, secure as being free from anxiety, safe as being sheltered from peril. So, for instance, the people of that secluded little town of Laish, whose peaceful existence amidst warlike neighbors is described with such singular beauty in the Book of Judges, are said to "dwell *careless*, quiet, and *secure*." The former phrase is literally "in trust," and the latter is "trusting." The idea sought to be conveyed by both seems to be that double one of quiet freedom from fear and from danger. So, again, in Moses' blessing, "The beloved of the Lord shall dwell *in safety* by Him," we have the same phrase to express the same twofold benediction of shelter, by dwelling in God, from all alarm and from all attack:

> "As far from danger as from fear,
> While love, almighty love, is near."

This thought of the victory of faith over fear is very forcibly set forth in a verse from the Book of Proverbs, which in our version runs "The righteous is bold as a lion." The word rendered "is bold" is that of our text, and would literally be "trusts," but obviously the metaphor requires such a translation as that of the English Bible. The word that properly describes the act of faith has come to mean the courage which is the consequence of the act, just as our own word *confidence* properly signifies trust, but has come to mean the boldness which is born of trust. So, then, the true way to become brave is to lean on God. That, and that alone, delivers from otherwise reasonable fear, and Faith bears in her one hand the gift of outward safety, and in her other that of inward peace.

Peter is sinking in the water; the tempest runs high. He looks upon the waves, and is ready to fancy that he is going to be swallowed up immediately. His fear is reasonable if he has only the tempest and himself to draw his conclusions from. His helplessness and the scowling storm together strike out a little spark of faith, which the wind cannot blow out, nor the floods quench. Like our Psalmist here, when Peter is afraid, he trusts. "Save, Lord, or I perish." Immediately the outstretched hand of his Lord grasps his, and brings him to safety, while the gentle rebuke, "O thou of little faith, wherefore didst thou doubt?" infuses courage into his beating heart. The storm runs as high as ever, and the waves beat about his limbs, and the spray blinds his eyes. If he leaves his hold for one moment down he will go. But, as long as he clasps Christ's hand, he is safe on that heaving floor as if his feet were on a rock; and as long as he looks in Christ's face and leans upon His upholding arm, he does *not* "see the waves boisterous," nor tremble at all as they break around him. His fear and his danger are both gone, because he holds Christ and is upheld by Him. In this sense, too, as in many others, "this is the victory that overcometh the world, even our faith."

NOTES

NOTES

NOTES

When Fears Transcend

William E. Sangster (1900-1960) was the "John Wesley" of his generation as he devoted his life to evangelism and the promotion of practical sanctification. He pastored in England and Wales, and his preaching ability attracted the attention of the Methodist leaders. He ministered during World War II at Westminster Central Hall, London, where he pastored the church, managed an air-raid shelter in the basement, and studied for his Ph.D. at the London University! He served as president of the Methodist Conference (1950) and director of the denomination's home missions and evangelism ministry. He published several books on preaching, sanctification, and evangelism, as well as volumes of sermons.

This message comes from *He Is Able*, published in 1936 by Hodder and Stoughton, London.

William E. Sangster

12

WHEN FEARS TRANSCEND

In the morning thou shalt say, Would God it were even! and at even thou shalt say, Would God it were morning! for the fear of thine heart wherewith thou shalt fear, and for the sight of thine eyes which thou shalt see (Deuteronomy 28:67).

PSYCHOLOGISTS HAVE OFTEN warned us against our misuse of the word "fear." They accuse laymen of speaking of it as an instinct whereas, of course, it is an instinctive emotion. They convict us of regarding it as a foe while all the time it is a friend. "If we only understood the service fear renders," they say, "we would never speak of it as any enemy again."

It is well to bear the warning in mind. Simple fear has been a faithful servant of mankind through all the long development of our race. Fear warns us against danger and checks impetuosity. Fear begets a proper care. Fear is the most efficient policeman on our traffic congested streets; it compels caution and preserves life. No man is without fear. If such a man should be born, he would be a danger to the whole community and a just object of dread.

Fear of the consequences is not the highest motive in rejecting evil but it is a very common one, and a buttress of morality not to be despised. In the hour of swift temptation, when desire and opportunity exactly coincide, many men have been distressed to discover that the love of virtue was not strong enough of itself to keep them in the paths of purity, but the fear of being found out checked the passionate impulse and saved them from disaster. None can doubt that fear is often a friend.

But it is a foe as well. Fear so soon becomes morbid. It ceases to be a cautionary mood and grows into a bogey that haunts the mind and finally enslaves the whole personality. It builds national barriers and piles up armaments. It hinders peace. It fosters racial hatred and plagues the individual life as well. Fear takes many forms. The fear of destitution haunts the honest poor. The fear of failure ploughs furrows in the face of business men. The fear of age fills the waiting rooms of plastic surgeons. The fear of death is almost as wide as mankind.

Can Jesus deal with fear? Is He able to deliver men and women from the paralyzing perturbations which make so many lives a burden? We answer without hesitation that He is able. There are no more exultant people in the army of the redeemed than those who have been saved from fear. "To be saved from the extremities of fear," they say, "is to be saved from hell."

A Pardonable Exaggeration

So impressed are some people with the evil character of fear that they are disposed to make it the arch-demon of all life and they say, "There is nothing to fear but fear." It is an exaggeration but the exaggeration is pardonable. Many of our fears have no basis in reality. They are the home-made products of over-anxious hearts and as unsubstantial as the Specter on the Brocken. The Brocken is the highest point of the Hartz Mountains in Germany. For centuries it was a place of dread because of the giant who lived upon its top. Many times had the giant been seen. Credible witnesses solemnly swore that they had watched him, and people avoided the mountain as a place too dangerous to approach.

But with the advance of learning thoughtful men grew skeptical about the giant and made investigations. And this is what they found. They found that reliable witnesses had seen the giant only at sunrise or sunset—i.e. when the sun's rays were horizontal. They found also that he only appeared when the Brocken was free of cloud and when its neighbors were covered with mist, and they guessed the truth at once. The ghostly and terrifying specter which the traveler sees upon the sky is nothing but a magnified and distorted image of himself. He trembles at his own reflection. He flies at his own shadow.

He thinks he is being pursued by monstrous and uncanny fiends, but he is being dogged by nothing but a diseased imagination. *Some* of our terrors are like that. They are simply not real. They are conceived and brought forth and nurtured in fear. Jesus sweeps that litter from our minds. The Specter on the Brocken disappears when the wild disperses the mist or the sun mounts higher. So do these unsubstantial fears vanish when the wind of the Spirit blows through them and the Sun of Righteousness appears. Have faith. "Fear knocked at the door, fear opened it and lo, there was no one there."

But not all our fears are unsubstantial. Fears are sometimes fostered by facts. A man living on the slopes of a volcano and constantly reminded of his peril by a pall of smoke and the shuddering earth has something more to fear than fear. He has facts to fear as well. Many people live in the shadow of ugly facts and their fears have an undeniable core of truth.

Some Common Fears

Let us look at some of the common fears that not unnaturally haunt the minds of men and which are more than mere bogies and phantoms.

There is the fear of *want.* How common this is and how old! Men have grappled with the fear of want from the dim dawn of history and, in this age of commercial depression, an immense multitude grapple with it still. Only those who have lived the life know the dread insecurity of living on an uncertain pittance, and the nightmare that life becomes unless those fears can be killed by perfect trust in the love of God.

Jesus met the anxious poor men of His day by pointing to the birds and flowers. "Behold the birds of the heaven that they sow not neither do they reap, nor gather into barns and your heavenly Father feedeth them." "Consider the lilies of the field how they grow; they toil not neither do they spin. Yet I say unto you that even Solomon in all *his* glory was not arrayed like one of these." So our Lord drew the inference. If God feeds the birds and clothes the flowers He will feed and clothe His human children, who are of more value than birds and flowers. And seed-time and harvest have not failed. Though "man's inhumanity to man makes countless thousands mourn," God has been faithful. His general providence and His particular care have been constant through the ages.

Many are the incidents in the garner of one's own experience that confirm the promise. I have seen the strangest fulfillments of this word. Sometimes the answer to prayer has been so singular in its attention to detail that one could barely refrain from laughing, as Sarah laughed and St. Teresa and Henrietta Soltau. I remember the old saint who had been a nurse in an aristocratic family but found her pension insufficient after the war. One week she had to meet a bill of several pounds and had not so much as a shilling towards it. The thought of debt was dreadful to her and she begged God to undertake the burden and give her a settled mind. And, as she read the scriptures, a great peace fell upon her heart with the words "Thou shalt have plenty of silver." Somehow she felt they were meant for her. She even declined a pound note on the day before the bill was due because she could not feel that it was God's way to help. Then, in the hour of her need, when to some of her friends she seemed certain of disillusionment and not a little obstinate, her faith was triumphantly vindicated by the part repayment of a loan she had made to a neighbor years before and the very memory of which had almost slipped from her mind. The amount was placed in her hand by an apologetic woman who begged to be excused for the delay and explained that only the most rigorous economy in her household had made possible the saving of an occasional coin. "Thou shalt have plenty of silver."

The old nurse laughed to save herself from crying but the smiles and tears were all of joy.

Nor is that incident singular. Any man with ten years' experience of the care of souls could take out of his memory a group of little incidents of singular providence, differing in detail and sometimes so odd as almost to demand an apologetic preface, but *true*, as true as God and His love, and not easily waved aside as mere coincidences. For the most part they seem to come to people of great faith whose prayers are not compact of just petitions and who are very far from thinking of God only when they want something. But they witness impressively to God's personal care of His children and foster the faith in us which banishes fear.

The recurrent needs of every day are all known to God. A full reliance can be put upon His promises. Many people know nothing of these extremities of need and must find God's providence work for them in ordered and unspectacular ways, but those who live on the lip of want may have this precious compensation that, again and again, from behind a frowning providence, clearer than their neighbors, they see His smiling face.

Another Common Fear

Or take another common fear—the fear of *bereavement*. This is an inevitable sorrow of life. All who live for any length of days come to a dark hour in a cemetery and follow as much as is mortal of someone dear to them. It is hard to keep this dread at bay because we know it is sure. I have a friend whose mother died when he was small and who is devoted to his father. His father grows old. Every new year my friend confesses to this fear. "I keep wondering," he says, "if father will be spared to me another year."

All folk know this fear in some form. Sometimes we pick up a newspaper and read of a terrible accident and the thought shapes itself in our mind, "if that had been my wife . . . or my child . . ." and we put the paper down and think quickly of something else because our heart has turned sick inside us. The fear of bereavement is ugly, intrusive, and terrifying.

But, if bereavement is inevitable, we need not anticipate it. It would be the height of folly to mortgage the joys of halcyon days by importing a woe that may be far distant, and even if signs follow swift upon our fears and convince us that events will soon confirm our worst forebodings we still have securest refuge in the everlasting love of God. There is a special grace for a special need. That grace is not given with our anticipations: it is given only with the *event*.

Nor must the ground of this great confidence be confused with optimism. Mere optimism is a shallow delusion of the mind, absurdly over-praised. I remember once going to a family every member of which had been stunned by a sudden and awful bereavement and, try as I would, I could not pass God's comfort on. The words seemed to die upon my lips and finally I murmured something about coming back later in the day, and I left the house. And at the corner of the street I saw a chirpy "wayside pulpit." It said, "Cheer up! It may never happen." I answered it back. I said, "It's happened." In a dazed way I kept repeating, "It's happened."

There is no lift in optimism in an hour like that. Like the nerveless needle of a broken barometer it continues to point, even in a thunderstorm, to "very fair." It keeps saying "Cheer up! It may never happen," and is utterly dumb when it does happen. The religion of Jesus says "Even if it does happen—what then?" "Yea, though I walk through the valley of the shadow of death, I will fear no evil: for *Thou* art with me."

Or take the fear of *age*. Folk often confess that this is one of their worst bogies, and we all know people who are oppressed with the swift passage of time. I worked once with a man whose only reading matter was a book called *How Not to Grow Old*. His pathetic attempts to make a little hair go a long way and his childish glee if someone guessed him a couple of years younger than he was, were pitiful to behold. He grew old rapidly. He was too anxious about it to keep young. Anxiety ages. His methods defeated their own ends like the usher in court who shouts "Silence! Silence!" and makes more noise than anybody else.

Yet there is a deep and serious undertone in all this. Nobody wants to be a burden to others. Life grows wearisome to those whose powers are failing, and though we would never admit that our aged dear ones are a burden to us, we *do* find ourselves forging the hope that we shall not be a burden to those who come after us. Let us take refuge still in the love of God. Observations go to prove that it is possible to grow old gracefully and God has some rich compensations for His ripe saints.

Even when sight grows dim and hides the sacred page, and hearing fails and public worship is closed as a channel of grace, He has His own secret ways of feeding our souls. I heard recently of a young man who had been in great trouble. His wife had gone blind. While her sun was still climbing the sky it was blotted from the heavens and midnight descended before it was noon. Her chief delight in life had been their lovely garden; all her leisure was given to the cultivation of flowers and no small part of her bitterness arose from the thought that the garden had gone from her forever.

But her devoted husband has tried to give her the garden again and in a novel way. He has taken up all the plants that were there merely for their looks, and he has replaced them by plants whose chief merit is their smell. Out with the aster and in with the thyme. Out with the peonies and in with lavender. Out with the marguerites and in with stock, pinks, and carnations. Out with the rhododendrons and in with more roses. And my last news of that heroic couple is that the wife has her garden again and her husband has the joy of giving it to her. By another sense she retains her own. Books are closed and life in the house grows irksome but spring in the garden is still precious though the joy of it comes another way.

That seems to me to be a parable of the way God deals with His aged saints when their powers begin to decay. He finds a secret stair to their soul. He is constant when other joys have fled and He tells them things He does not tell to us. I am not disposed to dread old age when the saints open to me the treasury of their God-given wisdom.

Let the last word be about the fear of *death*. Few people are entirely ignorant of this fear in some form or other. Sometimes it is the physical fact of dying. Sometimes it is just regret at leaving so much that we have found beautiful and good. The thought of judgment is terrifying to others, while some shrink at the mere mystery of the vast unknown. If all these fears are matted together in one mind it invests the thought of death with unutterable dread.

On June 5, 1910, O. Henry, the famous short story

writer, lay dying. As the shades of death gathered about him, he said to the nurse, "Nurse, bring me a candle." "A candle?" she said. "Why do you want a candle?" "Because," he answered grimly, "I'm afraid to go home in the dark."

Many people dread the path that leads out of this earthly life because it seems all dark. For them the great question remains

> "Whether 'tis ampler day divinelier lit
> Or homeless night without;
> And whether stepping forth, my soul shall see
> New prospects, or fall sheer—a blinded thing!
> *There* is, O grave, thy hourly victory,
> And there, O death, thy sting."

But think a moment. If God is our Father (and Jesus said He is): if we are among those to whom He gave power to become the sons of God in all the richness of that relationship, and if death is but the summons to His more immediate presence, what room is there for fear? Most of us know that when we came into *this* world we were not unexpected and we were not unwelcome. Loving hands had made joyous preparation for our coming and warm arms held us tenderly against a warm bosom. Will our Heavenly Father be less kind to us than our earthly mother? Is the love and hospitality of this poor earth more cordial than the raptured greetings of heaven? We cannot think it. "Perfect love casts out fear." "Love in its fullness drives all dread away."

We can but give the gifts He gave, and plead His love for love.

NOTES

The Courage of Religion

James Moffatt (1870-1944) was born and educated in Scotland and is best remembered as a gifted teacher and New Testament scholar. Ordained in 1896, he pastored two churches in Scotland, taught Greek and New Testament exegesis at Mansfield College, Oxford (1911-1915), and taught church history at the United Free Church College in Glasgow (1915-1927). He published the New Testament section of his *New Translation* in 1913 and the Old Testament section in 1924. The complete Bible in one volume was issued in 1926. He served as professor of church history at Union Seminary, New York, from 1927 to 1939, during which time he published a number of scholarly works.

This sermon is taken from *A Treasury of the World's Great Sermons*, published by Kregel Publications.

James Moffatt

13

THE COURAGE OF RELIGION

And David said in his heart, I shall now perish one day by
the hand of Saul (1 Samuel 27:1).

BUT HE DID not perish by the hand of Saul. He lived to
pronounce a eulogy, and a generous eulogy, upon his dead
foe. Saul perished first; his attack seemed irresistible, but
it came to nothing, and David's fear proved vain.

Thus do even strong, religious natures often make
trouble for themselves out of a future about which they
know next to nothing. David was terribly discouraged at
this moment. The fond hope which he had cherished of
succeeding to a high position in the kingdom had ebbed
away. Wherever he turned, he saw nothing but the
prospect of further peril and privation, whose end, sooner
or later, meant defeat. Saul's resources were so numerous,
and his power was so versatile, that the result of the
struggle seemed to David to be merely a question of
time.

Now, forethought is one thing. We have to be on the
alert against the risks of life and open-eyed in face of any
horrible combination which may threaten our position or
affect our interests injuriously. But it is another thing
altogether to collapse weakly in despair of heart before
apprehensions and anxieties which may turn out to be
quite unfounded. In the early part of the last century a
young scientist once wrote: "It has been a bitter
mortification to me to digest the conclusion that the race
is for the strong, and that I shall practically do little more
but be content to admire the strides others make in
science." It was Charles Darwin. He was in bad health,
and bad health is apt to bring low spirits. Yet Darwin
lived to do work which made others only too glad to follow
his strides in science. That is one instance of the

misjudgments which we are prone to make about our future, and David's bitter cry is just another.

Dealing with Depression

We can all see how wrong it is for a religious man to yield thus to depression, and how foolish this perverse habit is, but surely we can also feel how natural it is to lose heart and courage for the moment. Only those who have had to make the effort know how difficult it is to be brave at certain times in life. I am speaking not of the courage required for some enterprise or heroic action, but of the quieter courage which holds depression at bay, which braces the soul against anxiety and which enables people to be composed and firm under circumstances of hardship, when doubts as to our own usefulness and prospects occur, or when the pressure of things seems to thwart and even to deny any providence of God within our sphere of life. At such moments, the strain almost overpowers us. David was living the anxious life of a hunted creature, like Hereward the Wake, or Bruce in the Athole country, or Wallace in Ayshire and the North, obliged to be on his guard against repeated surprises, his nerves aquiver with the tension of pursuit. As he bitterly complained, Saul was chasing him like a partridge among the hills. True, he had first succeeded in outwitting his foe, but at night reaction came over him like a wave. How long could this guerrilla warfare go on? One day the fugitive pretender would be sure to fall into an ambush! He could not expect always to foil the attack of his enemies! And so thinking he lost his heart. "I shall now perish one day by the hand of Saul."

We must be on our guard against such moments of reaction, especially toward evening, when after the tiring day the body is too exhausted to help the mind against the inroad of oracle fears. Then doubts about our faith and health and work and income rise and shape themselves into dark possibilities of evil, and feelings are apt to get the better of our self-possession, and faith is shaken for the moment. It is a great part of life's management to be on our guard against such apprehensions. Towards night, or when you are run down, whenever reaction sets in, the judgment and the content of faith are apt to be disturbed by fears which either vanish or at any rate shrink to their true proportions in the light of the morning. You are bound to remember that, and to lay your account with it.

The mood is almost constitutional with some. Owing to inherited disposition or to imperfect training, some are tempted to dwell repeatedly upon the darker side of things. They are highly strung, by nature. Their sensitive hearts get easily depressed. The sense of danger, which acts upon certain people like a pacific stimulus, only serves to damp their courage. They belong to the class for which Bunyan, with all the generosity of a strong nature, felt such evident sympathy—Mrs. Despondency, Miss Much-Afraid, Mr. Fearing, Mr. Feeble-Mind, the ready inaction of Faint Despair and of Castle Doubting.

At the same time, neither circumstances nor character can altogether explain the occasional failure of moral courage in life. David, for example, lived in the open air; his body was strong; there was nothing morbid about his habits of life; he loved music and fighting. But nevertheless he was subject to fits of depression and dismay, which discolored life and made God seem actually indifferent or hostile to him. Now, what is to be done, when the spirit is thus overwhelmed within us?

David's Example

In the first place, there is usually something that can be done. Action is one of the best means of banishing idle shadows from the path. There is this to be said for David, that he never allowed self-pity to benumb his faculties. Despair made him energetic; it drove him at this crisis to seek shelter outside the boundaries of the country for himself and his household. Instead of folding his hands and letting things drift, he did his best to secure a haven for his family and to provide as well as he could for himself. Such is the first note of practical courage in our religious life. Often to lose heart means, with us, to lose vigor. People brood on their difficulties and perplexities until hardship is allowed to paralyze their faculties of resistance.

Now David's example summons us to face our troubles and to make the best of them, instead of sitting down to bemoan ourselves as the victims of fate. We all have our moments of cowardice. Thank God if they are only moments. Thank God if we have enough faith and nerve left to rise, as David did, even with a heavy heart, and put our hand to some business of the day. The mere feeling of movement will help to raise our courage. It will inspire us with the conviction that we are not meant to be mere driftwood, at the mercy of the wild risks and chances of the current. Our very proverb about "rising to the occasion" is based upon this truth. And to rise to the occasion means that we shake off the selfish torpor of self-pity and depression, standing up to grapple somehow with the difficulties of our lot.

Feelings or Faith?

The second mark of returning courage is to get away from the circle of our own feelings, and this is the escape of faith. Remember what David forgot for the moment— God's purpose and God's faithfulness. Long ago he had been chosen from the sheepfold for a career which neither he nor anyone else anticipated. God had lifted him from the country to the court. His vocation had opened up, and now, although everything appeared to contradict this purpose, could it have failed? Could the will of God be shattered or recalled? Was the past experience of His favor accidental or delusive? Such is the heart's logic of the religious man.

It is in fact the underlying faith in providence which rallies and restores our nature in its broken hours. Newman once called it the true religion of Great Britain. "What Scripture illustrates from its first page to its last," he declared, "is God's providence; and that is nearly the only doctrine held with a real assent by the mass of religious Englishmen. Hence the Bible is so great a solace and refuge to them in trouble." The reason why people draw hope and encouragement in this way is that religion means not simply an ordered view of the universe, which excludes caprice and tyranny alike, but a sense of the divine control and care for the individual.

A vague impression of providence would not rally anybody. What is needed to reinforce our moral strength is the conviction of God's personal interest in the single life, and of a wise, loving Will which never fails anyone who loyally follows it at all hazards. No outsider can form any idea of the change produced in a human soul by this resolute trust in the higher responsibility of God. The center is changed from nervous worry about oneself to a pious reliance on the care of the Lord, and a real but unaccountable sense of security passes into the very secrets of the soul. According to our temperament it takes many forms, from quiet calm to an exulting confidence, but in every form this faith does its perfect work by putting the entire concern of life into God's sure keeping.

Here, then, lies another remedy for nervousness and agitation about our prospects. Even in your hours of panic, when life seems brought to nothing, you can reflect: "After all, I am the object of my Father's care and purpose. I can trust Him absolutely. He has put me here and been with me hitherto. I am not left to myself. I cannot, I will not, believe that He has grown weary of the responsibility for what He made." To say that in your heart is not vanity; it is the sheer trust of faith, won from long experience and still to be verified during the days to come. Unknown as your future may be, you are at the disposal of One whom you have learned to trust, whose management of life you are prepared to accept, not coldly but with a steady and even a cheerful consent. The deepest thing you know about your life is that you are His choice and charge and handiwork.

The Greatness of Gratitude

That naturally opens out into a third source of courage, namely, gratitude. Faith, in order to do its perfect work, needs to pass from dull submission and acquiescence into a habit of thankfulness to God. The spirit of praise ministers to our sense of God's reality by calling up before our mind and heart those acts in which we see His character and from which we are intended to gain a firmer impression of His continuous and personal interest in ourselves. When we thank God, we realize Him more profoundly and intimately than ever. Too often, I am afraid, most of us are thankful to get past some difficulty, and if we remember it at all it is to congratulate ourselves secretly upon the skill and good fortune which carried us over the jolt in the road. But these steps and stages should be precious to the soul. They ought to be accumulating for us, as the years go by, a steady faith in God's sure faithfulness. Now that is impossible unless we are in the habit of saying to ourselves, as each favor comes: "This is the doing of God. I thank thee for this my Father. Thou art very good to me."

Dejection is frequently the result of nothing more than a failure to practice this habit of thankfulness. We forget to praise God for His daily mercies, and so they pass away from us without leaving any rich deposit of assurance, as they would have done if we had owned His hand in every one. Now the full good of any deliverance and help is not merely the outward benefit which it confers upon our life. The relief is something. But surely we are also intended to win from it a new confirmation of our faith in God's character and a deeper apprehension of His purpose in relation to ourselves. The repeated acts of God within our personal experience are so many glimpses into the constancy and truth of His will, and it is our privilege to use those, from time to time, in order to learn how surely He can be depended upon.

David seems to have forgotten this, for the time being. He had rejoiced over his recent exploit, but he had not allowed it to bear home to him the sense of God's unfailing care, and that was one reason why he lay open to misgivings and fear. It is always so, in human experience, when we face the future without having won from the past a more settled faith in the continuity of God's living will.

Kinds of Courage

Such are some of the methods by means of which religion ministers to strength and constancy of life. Courage indeed varies with our disposition and our training. "The French courage," Byron wrote once to Murray, "proceeds from vanity, the German from phlegm, the Turkish from fanaticism and opium, the Spanish from pride, the English from custom, the Dutch from obstinacy, the Russian from insensibility, but the Italian from anger." A generalization like this is always loose, but it serves to remind us how many forces in life will call out courage; an inspiring example, sympathy, indignation, pity, the sense of self-respect—any of these will often keep us from breaking down and giving way. Faith can pour strength along these and other channels, but most directly of all it helps us, if it is real, to be self-possessed and brave by calling up before us the entire compass of the situation. Where we fail is in forgetting to include the greatest element of all or in undervaluing it. We leave God out of our estimate. David said, "I shall now perish one day by the hand of Saul." Was there no more in his life than that? I and Saul? What about God? Had life resolved itself into a mere trial of strength between David and his foe? Was there no longer any providence in it? What of the splendid confession before Goliath, "The Lord who delivered me from the power of the lion and the bear will deliver me out of the hand of this Philistine"? Ah, there spoke the true David, the man after God's own heart, who recognized God's hand in the action and passion of his days, and who was no more sure of his own existence than of God's answer to the faith and effort of the soul.

The sterling courage of religion is to be satisfied with this assurance, to win it from experience and to hold it by due care of the mind and body and by a habit of sincere thankfulness to God. It may be that for a time your life is very different from what you expected. You may have to face difficult passages and dark turns when it is not easy to feel much more than the annoyance and uncertainty and strain that sometimes crowd upon you with disturbing force. There are days when you scarcely venture to look ahead, in case you are unnerved by the prospect. It seems as if almost everything conspired to strip life of its just hope and vitality. When such clouds of physical reaction and brain-weariness come down, will you believe that God has not abandoned you? Do not reckon up nervously this chance and that, pitting the one against the other, but fall back on what you know of God's character and goodness in the past, till His word and witness put some fresh hope into your soul.

> Say not, The struggle naught availeth,
> The labor and the wounds are vain;
> The enemy faints not, nor faileth
> And as things have been, they remain;

say it not, even in your heart. Believe it not. What does remain is the undying interest of God in you. What faints not, nor faileth, is this redeeming purpose. Don't give way. Whatever you do, do not lose heart and hope, under the gray sky. Tell yourself to wait, to wait for the living God, and see. And you will see what thousands of men and women have rejoiced to see, that, whoever fails you, whatever may be thrust on you or taken from you, nothing, neither life nor death, nor things present, nor things to come, will be able to separate you from the love of God which is in Christ Jesus, our Lord.